Kate'sCakeDecorating

APPLE

Kate'sCakeDecorating

Techniques and Tips
for Fun and Fancy Cakes
for All Occasions

KATE SULLIVAN

Cake designer and founder of New York City's Amazing
LovinSullivanCakes

Photographs by Gabrielle Revere

Published in the UK in 2004 by
Apple Press
Sheridan House
112-116A Western Road
Hove BN3 1DD
UK

www.apple-press.com

ISBN 1-84092-471-3

10 9 8 7 6 5 4 3 2 1

Design: Yee Design
back cover image, left: holger thoss

Printed in China

CONTENTS

The Cakes

INTRODUCTION

Many expert cake decorators come to their craft because they love to bake and want to adorn their delicious creations as beautifully as possible, especially if they're cooking for a wedding or special event.

Not me.

I got started as a complete novice to baking. I turned to icing—fondant, ganache, and buttercream—because I wanted to sculpt in a new form and I loved the idea of feeding my art to people—especially my friends and family. I wasn't expecting to end up in love with cakes—the tiny little impacts of aroma and the textures underneath the decorations make my heart swoon. But my love for a perfect curling wave breaking on top of a meringue is now equaled by the amount of love I secretly drop into my recipes when I cook.

I see every component of cake as fair game for interpretation: Chilled firm cake can be cut, molded, shaped, carved, and put back together again with buttercream to create a shape that isn't just a cake, but a sculpture. I can affix a marzipan accordion to a ceramic bride-and-groom cake topper for my friend Joe's wedding cake. A Vegas marquee can shine in silver for (one of!) my own wedding cakes.

I've found that no matter what I want to do, there's some form of pliable sugar product out there that can become almost any shape or texture. Some of these products, such as marzipan and gum paste, are sort of like Play-doh (but unlike Play-doh, they're actually intended to be eaten). Royal icing can flow smoothly and then harden into whimsical fine lines of words hovering like lace above the surface of a cake. Or form velvety roses. Or sheets of smooth and shiny porcelain-like shapes.

It takes some time (really, a long time) to make and decorate a cake, and some of this stuff is ridiculously painstaking, but if there's some part of you that can actually see the appeal of basket-weaving with icing or sculpting a cake, then you'll understand what I mean.

There's this great, magical novel (and movie) called *Like Water for Chocolate* by Laura Esquivel. Her main character, Tita, infuses the food she prepares not only with amazing and exotic flavors like rose petals, but with her own very powerful emotions, which then pass into whoever eats them.

When Tita's tears fall into the wedding cake batter created for a pair of ill-fated lovers, the wedding party eats the cake and is overcome with unexplainable sadness. I always think of Tita when I work on a cake and I psychically pour love and happiness into a recipe, hoping that love will become contagious to the eater.

Even when someone has no idea what went into making a special cake for him or her, that person definitely instinctively understands that a lot of your spirit ends up in there. And, the more personal you can make a cake, the more it means to that individual, because then he or she knows you designed the cake with him or her in mind.

I love the process of designing and creating cakes, and the moment someone sees his or her cake for the first time is priceless. No matter who or how old they are, people get the same look on their face as when they were about five years old and were confronted with a mass of sugar with their name piped across it.

Of course, in some cases, the cake will have been created for a five-year-old—and that look is even more amazing!

No matter what the age, this rule applies universally: in every culture, food equals love, so basically, this book is about love. And cake. Clearly, the two go hand in hand.

CHAPTER

1

Getting Started

HOW TO USE THIS BOOK

The beginning of this book is about the nuts and bolts of making and decorating a cake. If you've never constructed an elaborate cake before, spend some time with the introductory chapters. Get a sense of the tools and ingredients. Practice techniques like piping an icing pattern or shaping a gum paste flower before you use them on the cake itself.

I can't stress too strongly the importance of being organized. It makes a big difference if you start the decorating process with your tools and colors at hand, and the components of the cake prepared in advance. This first chapter, "Getting Started," will tell you how to stay on top of the job, rather than letting it overwhelm you.

The Supplies and Tools section (page 15) will tell you what you need to complete each step of the cake...or, at least, what will make the job easier. (I'd been covering cakes with fondant just fine for years before I'd noticed a tool called an icing smoother. Once I used it, I just loved it, and now I never do the fondant without it.)

You need a large, clean work surface and you have to stay on top of the many messes: it's very distracting to have the bowls of icing still on your work surface when you're moving on to the decorating stage. Creating a Work Space (page 14) describes methods of making the most of your cake-making environment.

If you decide you'd like to personalize any details of the cakes in this book or design your own cake, Planning and Designing Your Cake (page 12) will help guide you to your personal best.

Many steps are repeated from cake to cake: baking and filling the cake, covering it with fondant. You'll find all of these in chapter 2, Basic Instructions. Since all the individual cake's instructions start with a cake that's already baked, filled, and iced, this chapter will guide you through that process. Once you get to the individual cakes, there'll be a lot of detailed how-tos, but these chapters will also sometimes refer you back to Basic Instructions.

Here's where it really all started for me, as well as for a generation of girls in the '60s. Ah, the excitement of firing up that little light bulb; I just never got it out of my blood!

...

At the heart of the book are the instructions for decorating specific cakes, categorized by design themes. The cakes are listed in each chapter in order of difficulty, starting with the easiest. This is somewhat subjective; for instance, if your piping expertise outshines your modeling skills, you may not agree with the ordering of all the cakes. At the end of The Cakes portion of this book, there's a gallery of photographs to show how the techniques I've just discussed can be adapted to create different designs. There are also photographs showing how you can make variations on some of the cakes, such as changing the size or adding a cake topper. These should help you visualize ways to customize the cakes for your own events.

At the end of the book, I've set out some recipes for baking good, sturdy, delicious cake. You can substitute your own recipe, as long as it's a cake that holds its shape. I've also included calculation tables so you can figure out the number of servings based on cake size (page 125) and the amount of fondant you will need to cover your cake (page 127). You'll also find templates for tracing shapes and patterns. The Sources section will suggest places where you can buy the specialized equipment that you may need.

One last word: Everything I know about cake making I learned from books like this one. I've discovered that no two books agree about every technique, so I've developed my methods from taking the things I've read and adapting them to what best suits me. These techniques aren't gospel; if you find an easier or better way, that's great!

Planning and Designing Your Cake

PLANNING

Making and decorating cakes almost always take longer than I think they will. Even after ten years of cake making, I'm still surprised at how many late nights I spend working to finish up a project that I thought would be done the day before. For tiered cakes, I always observe a minimum three-day rule. It's a good idea to use this as a starting point and then figure out your own stride as you become more experienced.

Day one: bake and cool the cakes, and work on any decorations that can be made in advance. Day two: fill and cover the cakes and continue with the decorations. Day three: put it all together. If the cake has a lot of decorations, or if they're especially complex, you may want to start way in advance. I always do as much as I can a week or two ahead. That way, if something breaks or it doesn't turn out the way I had hoped, I have time to fix it or do it over again.

I've learned through experience not to cut corners on certain steps. When I first started, I would quickly fill cakes with a layer of icing, then immediately cover them with fondant, only to watch the fondant buckle when its weight started to press the filling out from the sides of the cake. It would make me want to cry. The importance of details like letting the filling set or giving the fondant time to dry becomes painfully clear the first time you ignore them.

You should also calculate the time you put your cakes in the oven backward from the cooling time. Since cake making used to be a moonlighting activity for me, it would regularly be 9:00 at night before I got a cake into the oven, which meant that I'd have to stay up until 1 AM or later before the cake was cool enough to wrap up and refrigerate. Some cakes take a lot of time to mix and to bake, especially bigger cakes or ones with many tiers. As any experienced baker knows, oven temperatures vary from unit to unit, so any cake may take more or less time to bake than stated in the recipe.

Good planning really does make all the difference. Read the entire recipe through before starting and make sure you have all the ingredients and supplies called for, because those extra trips to the market really add up. Even worse is discovering, after you've gotten started, that you can't even get a missing item. Practice techniques like icing or sculpting with marzipan paste before you use them on the cake itself.

DESIGNING

Once you have the basics under your belt and have mastered a few techniques, you may want to design your own cakes. Use the cakes in this book to serve as springboards for your own ideas. An original creation, of course, requires just as much—if not more—planning as following the instructions in a book. For me, step one is to make a sketch. Even though the finished product may have evolved into something that bears just a fleeting resemblance to this initial visualization, it's useful to have the picture in front of me while I'm planning the cake.

A good way to envision the basic outline of a tiered cake is to take pans of the size and shape you're considering, stack them on top of each other, then step back and see if they really work together. This is particularly easy if you have a baking supply store near you: you can choose from a wide selection of pans before making any commitments. Remember that your tiers will usually be 3 to 4 inches (8 to 10 cm) tall, and the most common pans are 2 inches (5 cm) tall. You can use two 2-inch-tall pans per tier, in order to get the most accurate picture. Some cake supply stores will even have dummy cakes made out of Styrofoam. (These are used both for photo shoots and to augment real cakes if you want a really big cake, but don't need that many servings.) If your store has dummy cakes, they're even better than cake pans at helping you visualize the final product.

Consult the instructions in this book for techniques. For example, if you want to make a cake in the shape of a goldfish bowl, you could draw from the Ella Fant Dance cake (page 41), for the sphere and the Cuppa Joe to Go (page 110) for the top rim. Instead of a marzipan elephant balancing on top of a ball,

Daisy's Cake

* EDGE FLOWERS IN GOLD
TOP: DOG WOOD FLOWERS;
BRANCH. SILVER DREGEES
8" SQUARE TIER X4
SIDES - SMALL (BLOSSOMS)

CENTER: 12x & HEX
GOLD POMEGRANATES
SILVER DREGEE CENTERS

BOTTOM: LARGE PETAL
TIER. GOLD + SILVER
DETAILING - GOLD LEAVES
DREGEES OR BEADS

(POPPY PODS)

CAKE SUPPLY STORE
. STICK 5M. ROLLING PIN
+ FS PAPER
CATHERINE + SLAM'S (BIG FAT) WEDDING CAKE

HEART MADE OUT OF MARZIPAN
TO LOOK LIKE MADE OF BRANCHES.
(BROWN BARK)

BUTTERFLY
BUTTERFLY (RED)

OFF WHITE
FONDANT
ICING

POSSIBLY A BANNER?
(COULD SAY WHATEVER
YOU'D LIKE)

BRIDE & GROOM STANDING
IN FRONT OF HEART

BORDERS OF TINY
WILD FLOWERS AND BERRIES
AND LEAVES: BURGUNDY,
YELLOW, REDS, GREEN

FLOWERS FROM INVITATIONS
(CUT FLAT OUT OF ROLLED
SUGAR PASTE - OFF WHITE
W/ YELLOW CENTERS, GREEN
LEAVES)

LOVE BIRDS NESTLED IN BACK OF CAKE.

it could be a fish jumping up from its bowl or lounging on top. Maybe you'd like to make the Pom-Pom Luv Birds cake (page 38), but substitute the quilted fondant of the Blue Birds cake (page 48) for its basket weave. Or look at the Monkey Face Cake (page 57): with just a few modifications, it can easily be transformed into a bunny, bear, or kitty—in fact, any face at all—cake. The photographs in the gallery should be helpful in demonstrating how different techniques can be adapted for your own designs.

When you're constructing a cake from your own design, there's no single technique more useful than stepping back. Take a few steps away from your cake and look at it with a fresh eye. You may be inspired to move in an entirely new direction. Or you might have planned to add a hundred more details, but once you step back, it's clear that your cake is simply wonderful the way it is.

My most important advice of all: have fun!

Creating a Work Space

Since making a cake is a big undertaking, having an efficient, usable workspace is key. Rule one: you need at least one clear surface dedicated to cake making. You don't have to permanently reserve a corner of the kitchen for cakes, but for the length of the project, your cake-making space should be sacrosanct. It may mean giving the coffeemaker a new home for a few days, but it will make your job much easier in the long run.

For years, I worked out of my Brooklyn apartment kitchen, a 6-by-12-foot (1.8-by-3.6 m) area with a measly 4 feet (1.2 m) of counter space. I made just about as many cakes there as I do right now in a big kitchen filled with countertops, and it worked fine. But I had to stay focused. While I was working on a cake, the only things I'd allow on the countertop were my materials for the current step of the process. After I was done mixing the batter and frostings, the KitchenAid mixer would be whisked away to clear the surface for the next step. When the painting was done, I'd quickly clean the brushes and put the food coloring away in its box. And so on.

TIPS

Going into a cake project, be prepared for a surprising number of clean-ups! First, after the cake batters are made and in the oven, after they're out of their pans, after the icings are whipped up, and then after each separate phase of decoration. I always keep a sponge and a nice big stack of clean towels handy, and my attitude about it is ... there's something about having a blank canvas that makes all the difference.

In some ways, having a larger workspace presents its own challenge. There's always the temptation to let bowls and used equipment lie around. Bad idea! I've talked to other cake designers about this, and everyone agrees that no matter where you're working, a clear workspace is essential. A cluttered space can take the joy out of making a cake and turn it into drudgery. It can even affect the overall aesthetic results.

To work efficiently, you need to have your basic tools on hand. Certain basic kitchen supplies get used in every cake project: mixing bowls, a serrated knife, plastic wrap to cover icings and cakes in the refrigerator. On top of that, there are some decorating tools that will make your job easier and come up in just about every project in this book. Here's a list:

- **FOOD COLORING**
- **LEMON EXTRACT**
- **CORNSTARCH**
- **ICING BAGS AND COUPLERS**
- **CRAFT PAINTBRUSHES**
- **TOOTHPICKS**
- **TURNTABLE**
- **ROLLING PIN**
- **METAL SPATULAS**
- **RUBBER SPATULAS**
- **WAX PAPER**
- **SCISSORS**
- **ELECTRIC MIXER (PREFERABLY, A STANDING ELECTRIC MIXER)**
- **CAKE PANS**
- **CAKE BOARDS**

Before you start on a cake, you'll need to review its decoration and equipment list to make sure that you have whatever additional tools and supplies it requires. And check the recipe to make sure you have the groceries you'll need, such as flour, sugar, butter, and eggs, in the correct quantities for the number of tiers you'll be making.

Supplies and Tools

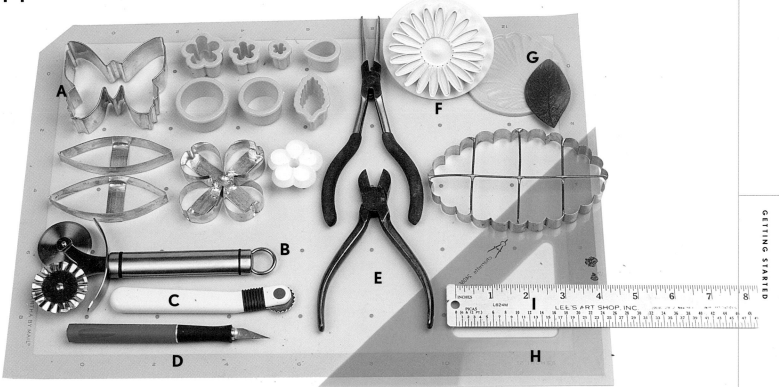

MEASURING AND CUTTING TOOLS

A | COOKIE AND GUM PASTE CUTTERS: These come in a variety of shapes and sizes, to create everything from flowers to dog bones. Traditionalists like metal cutters, but I've learned to love plastic because it doesn't rust.

B | PASTRY WHEEL: For trimming rolled fondant and cutting strips of gum paste.

C | TRACING WHEEL: Used for embossing quilt patterns into the fondant. Also, you can create a guideline by making a light run with a tracing wheel along the fondant surface.

D | CRAFT KNIFE: For cutting out template shapes and cardboard. You can even use it for trimming fondant and gum paste.

E | WIRE CUTTER AND NEEDLE-NOSE PLIERS: For cutting and bending cloth-covered wire.

F | PLUNGER FLOWER CUTTER: This will not only cut the shape of flower or leaf, but it will emboss a pattern onto flower or leaf. And it cleanly forces the gum paste or marzipan out onto your work surface.

G | VEINER: Available in plastic or rubber, this embosses veins into gum-paste flowers or leaves.

H | TRIANGLE: Architects use them for drawings, but cake makers can use them to create vertical and diagonal guidelines or quilted patterns.

I | METAL RULER: I find an 18-inch (45 cm) ruler (without cork backing) the most useful.

J | HOT GLUE GUN: Use it to attach cake boards to foam-core bases. When transporting a cake, just a few dots will attach each tier safely to its box. Also, I often use it to glue decorative ribbons to the base of a cake.

15

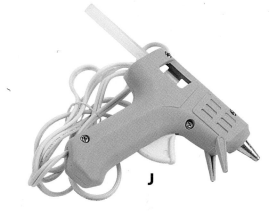

RIBBONS AND STRAIGHT PINS

I store ribbons and straight pins together—my own cake "sewing kit." The ribbons are used for decorating the edge of the foam-core base. Pins are essential for transferring patterns from templates onto cakes. You use them first to affix the template, then to draw the template shape in the fondant by marking holes. Although many people use roundhead pins, I use T-pins, which I find easier to hold comfortably. They're available at art-supply stores.

CAKE-FINISHING TOOLS

A | TURNTABLE: A sturdy metal turntable is a timesaver for the dedicated cake maker. It gives you easy access to all sides of the cake. This is especially useful when you're icing—you spin the turntable to ice the cake smoothly. If you make cakes only occasionally, though, you may want to use a less costly alternative, like an inexpensive plastic lazy Susan. Or you can just place the cake on a cake pan, and turn that.

B | PLASTIC SEPARATOR PLATES: For creating separated tiers. Each plate has four pegs for snapping in plastic pillars.

C | CARDBOARD CAKE BOARDS: You'll want cake boards, generally the size of the cake itself. These allow you to pick up a tier and move it around before the final assembly. Also, you can glue the bottom tier's cardboard to the cake base.

D | FOAM CORE CAKE BASE: Foam core provides a good base for the final cake. It's much stronger and less bendable than cardboard, so when you pick up the cake, it won't bow, and the fondant won't buckle.

E | MASONITE CAKE BOARD: An alternative to foam core. In some cases, it's aesthetically preferable, especially if you want the illusion of having no cake base—for instance, if you're serving the cake on a silver platter.

F | BENCH SCRAPER: An efficient tool for scraping off work surfaces covered with cornstarch or confectioner's sugar. With its straight edge, it can also be used for cutting and measuring.

G | ICING SMOOTHER: Smoothes the bubbles and bumps out of the surface of your fondant or sugar paste.

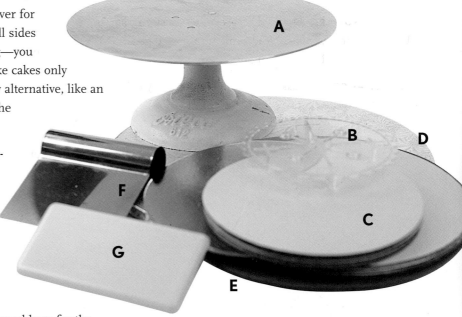

EDIBLE DECORATIONS

There are lots of packaged foods that serve as great cake decorations. Here's a sample (right):

A | SEMISWEET CHOCOLATE BLOCK: For making shaved chocolate curls.

B | SPRINKLES: These come in more shades than you'd imagine, from pastel to vibrant.

C | JORDAN ALMONDS: We've pictured silver-coated almonds, but they're available in a wide variety of colors.

D | COLORED SANDING SUGAR: A great way to create texture. Sanding sugar comes in a variety of grains, from coarse to very fine. You can color it yourself or buy it precolored.

E | SILVER DRAGÉES: Dragées come in different sizes and shapes, including ovals and hearts.

F | JELLYBEANS: Kids always love a jellybean border. On a more sophisticated cake, they can look like jewels.

G | CELERI SUGAR BEADS: If you search cake supply stores and online sources, you can find some unexpected gems. To me, these look like tiny pom-poms.

H | HEART ACCENTS: Cake supply stores carry tiny edible shapes to use as decorative accents—not just hearts, but stars, bunnies, and Halloween pumpkins.

I | LEMON: This is to represent the lemon extract that is used as the base for painting with powdered food colors. It smells

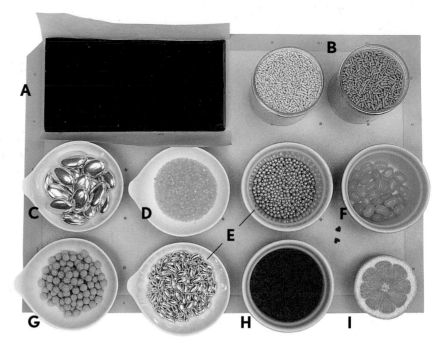

COLORING (LOWER LEFT)

A | POWDERS: Powdered colors, or dusts, are so dense, they're like using pigments. I like using them, mixed with lemon extract, to paint on the surface of the cake. There's an amazing range of custom-colored powders, available in petal, pearl, sparkle, and luster finishes. A less expensive option is using primary-color powders and mixing your own shades.

B | PASTES: The most concentrated of the liquid food colors. You mix these directly into your icings and sugar pastes, and a little goes a long way. Liquid or gel paste coloring is similar, but less intense.

C | PAINTBRUSHES: I like to get a package of craft brushes that includes flat and round soft brushes of different sizes. You can also get sable paintbrushes at an art-supply shop— a more expensive option, but the bristles stay on longer.

D | SPONGES: I like using these sea sponges—sold in art supply stores—but any clean new sponge will work to create texture.

E | FOOD-COLOR MARKERS: These are a relatively new thing for me, but I find them invaluable, especially for fine-line decorating. They're easier than the traditional pin method for stenciling a pattern onto a cake. And when you're drawing in details like little eyes onto molded characters, they give you more control than a paintbrush, and they do the job faster.

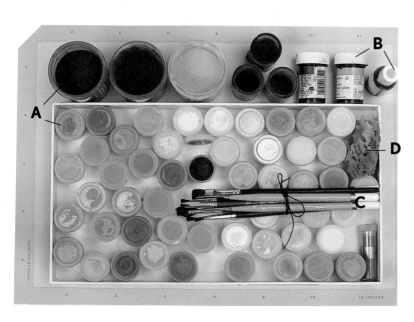

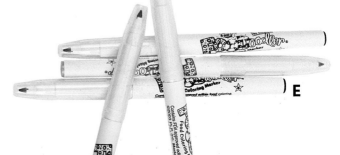

COOKING AND SHAPING TOOLS

A | ROLLING PIN: Because it's weighted, I love my metal rolling pin for rolling out fondant. Wooden rolling pins are great, too, but they take a little bit more elbow grease.

B | METAL SPATULA: Of all my spatulas, I reach for the 10-inch (25 cm) offset one the most. It's firm, yet flexible enough for icing and filling.

C | RUBBER SPATULA: For mixing icing, filling icing bags, and scraping down the sides of bowls.

D | GUM PASTE TOOLS: These modeling tools come with heads of different sizes and shapes. There are trumpet flower tools with cone-shaped heads, ball modeling tools, and veining tools for molding the shape of the petals and hollowing the centers of flowers.

E | TOOTHPICKS: Unbelievably helpful. I use them to add paste colors to icing, to mark the placement of decorations on the fondant, and to hold up marzipan or gum-paste decorations. When you're arranging dragées in a pattern, they're a great tool for the small detail work, fine-tuning placement, and making corrections.

F | WAX PAPER: Another underrated, essential tool. When you're making royal icing decorations in advance, you pipe them onto wax paper, which you peel off when you're ready to put the decorations on the cake.

G | SKEWERS: I use bamboo skewers to support decorations too large to rely on toothpicks.

H | STRAWS AND DOWELS: The supports for building a tiered cake. I prefer plastic straws because not only are they much easier to cut than wooden dowels, but, in my experience, they're just as strong.

I | CLOTH-COVERED WIRE: For the stems of gum-paste and royal-icing flowers. Cloth-covered wire comes in green and white, and in a range of thicknesses, from #20 (thickest) to #28 (thinnest) gauge. Like florist tape and stamens (below), this is available at florist- as well as cake-supply stores.

J | FLORIST TAPE: For covering cloth-covered wire. If you're making a sprig of flowers, you'll bind them together with the florist tape. Available in white, green, and brown.

K | STAMEN: A piece of stiff thread, with a ball at the end. Decorating stamens come with balls in different shapes and sizes. They are not edible.

L | GUM-PASTE ROLLING PIN: When you're working with gum paste and marzipan, it's on a much smaller scale than when you're rolling out fondant. This small plastic rolling pin is helpful.

M | GUM-PASTE CUTTING BOARD: The smooth surface and small size of this plastic cutting board make it ideal for rolling out gum paste and marzipan.

N | PASTRY BRUSH: Use this to whisk away the cornstarch after you've finished making gum-paste and marzipan decorations.

O | SILICONE BAKING MAT: Putting a nonstick mat in your cookie pan helps the cleanup process.

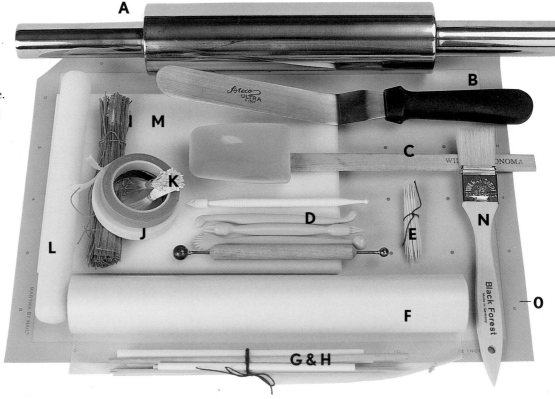

BAKING PANS

CAKE PANS: Professional, heavyweight pans conduct heat evenly and efficiently.

USEFUL TOOLS (not shown)

COLUMNS OR PILLARS: Used to support plastic separator plates, these are available in a variety of styles and sizes.

PASTRY BAGS: Some people prefer cloth bags for piping icing, but I find them a tremendous pain to clean. I use disposable 10-inch (25 cm) plastic bags, but lightweight polyurethane bags are a good alternative.

DECORATING TIPS: For piping icing, available in round, star, leaf, and basket-weave shapes. Of the hundreds of tips available, I gravitate toward #3 and #5 round tips most often.

COUPLERS: These allow you to change decorating tips on an icing bag.

FLOWER NAIL: Use it as a miniature turntable while you're making a royal icing flower.

MEASURING CUPS: Glass for liquids, metal for solids

MEASURING SPOONS

PAPER TOWELS: You'll use these not only for wiping up spills, but also wadded into little balls to make curved surfaces for drying gum-paste decorations.

PLASTIC WRAP: When you're storing icings, cakes, fondants, and gum paste, you need to keep them from drying out.

SERRATED KNIFE: Use it to slice a cake into layers.

SIEVE: I use it for sifting flour (it's easier to use than a sifter), and for dusting my work surface with cornstarch.

HEAVY-DUTY STANDING ELECTRIC MIXER: While it's possible to make elaborate cakes with a hand mixer, this makes the job a lot easier, especially when you consider some recipes call for mixing periods of five minutes or so.

WIRE COOLING RACKS: These are rectangular and round, and come in different sizes. I most often use a 12-inch (20 cm) round cooling rack, but for larger cakes, you need larger racks.

Basic Instructions

Even though the cake chapters in this book will guide you through each individual cake, there are some core techniques that remain the same for every cake you build. Almost all the cakes in this book will require the techniques I describe in the chapter that follows.

Before you start, some things should already be in place. First of all, you need to start with baked, cooled cakes. The colder the cake, the easier it is to handle and slice. I like to refrigerate my cakes for at least a couple of hours before I proceed.

Make sure you have everything you need for each step at hand before you start on it. I've listed everything you need at the beginning of each step; you can find details about specific tools in Supplies and Tools (page 15).

Slicing, Filling, and Coating a Cake

What you'll need:

Baked and chilled cakes (recipes page 123), long-blade serrated knife, cardboard cake boards (the same size as the cake), filling of your choice, rubber spatula, metal spatula, turntable

TIPS

◆ Most of the tiers are composed of two baked cakes of the same size, cut in half horizontally, filled with icing, and stacked into four layers. I make my cakes into a minimum of four layers per tier, but you can decide for yourself how many tiers you want. I find that four layers create a solid structure. Anything less becomes unstable when you're assembling the cake. Multiple layers (cemented together with icing) provide a good support for the heavy fondant and they strengthen the structure.

◆ If the cake comes out of the oven particularly uneven, use the serrated knife to trim the top off, making it level. If it's only slightly bowed, though, don't worry: you can compensate with the filling.

◆ Crumb coating is the base coat for the final icing, whether it's fondant, buttercream, or piped royal icing. Applying a thinned layer of icing to the top and sides of a filled cake seals it and prevents crumbs from marring the final icing. It also creates a smooth, level surface.

◆ Place a damp piece of paper towel under the cake board to prevent it from slipping and sliding on the turntable.

1. Dab a small amount of icing on a cake board and attach the bottom surface of one cake. Cut it into two layers, from $\frac{1}{2}$ inch (13 mm) to 1 inch (2.5 cm) thick, using the serrated knife, placing your hand on top of the cake to feel where the knife is going.

2. Take the layer you've sliced from the top, place it onto another cake board, and put it aside.

3. Fill the layers with your filling of choice—icing, ganache, preserves. In the picture, I've spread a layer of ganache, then a layer of icing. Use a rubber spatula to put a healthy dollop of the filling on the

cake, then spread it with a 10-inch (25 cm) metal spatula. If you've got a turntable, spin it as you spread to move the filling along and keep it even. Press the second layer down onto the first, using a cake board to help it adhere and keep it level. Repeat steps 1, 2, and 3 for the second cake, except this time, don't attach the bottom layer with icing to the cake board.

4. Ice the top of the first cake, then press the other cake down onto it. The original bottom of the second cake should now be on top.

5. Smooth out icing that oozes out the sides of the cake and fill in any gaps between the layers with icing. Cover the top and sides of the cake with a thin, smooth layer of icing to create a crumb coating (see "Tips" left). Refrigerate for about an hour to firm. A cake that's going to be covered in fondant needs only to be covered in this thin base layer of icing.

6. To frost a cake with buttercream, add icing to side of the cake with up-and-down strokes. Then smooth it out by holding the spatula perpendicular against the cake as you turn the turntable.

Working with Ganache

What you'll need: Ganache (page 127), rubber spatula, cake layers, mixing bowl, metal spatula, turntable

TIPS

◆ Ganache (page 27) is a great base coating (my favorite) for fondant-covered cakes because it can cover up myriad imperfections with a flawless and stable finish.

◆ Ganache is very easy to make, but very sensitive to temperature. At its thinnest it will be a liquid glaze, and at its thickest it will become stiff. Once you master keeping it at a creamy, spreadable thickness to work with, it's pure chocolate pleasure.

❖ If it's too thin, beat with a hand mixer. In hot weather, you may want to set aside a small amount of chilled ganache in the refrigerator; it can be added gradually to the warmer ganache as needed.

❖ If it begins to harden, heat in the microwave for 5 seconds at a time or over a double boiler until softened. Or, you can set aside some warmed ganache to add as needed.

◆ When spread on the outside of a cake it will set very rapidly. Work quickly and continually. Keep smoothing the surface as you work to make sure it doesn't set unevenly.

1. Start with ganache at a soft but dense, spreadable consistency.

2. Use a rubber spatula to put a healthy dollop of ganache on the cake (see Slicing, Filling, and Coating a Cake, page 22).

3. Spread with a 10-inch (25 cm) metal spatula.

Covering with Fondant

What you'll need: Fondant (page 128), cornstarch, rolling pin, filled and coated cake tier (see Slicing, Filling, and Coating a Cake, page 22), long serrated knife, icing smoother, cake board

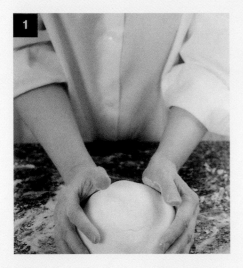

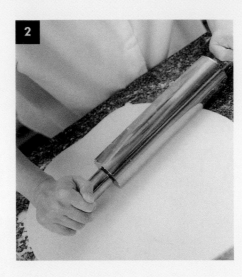

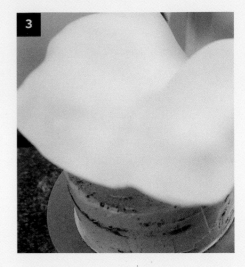

1. Before you start working with fondant, dust a clean work surface, your hands, and the rolling pin with cornstarch. Knead the fondant until it's pliable, then form it into a ball.

2. Roll fondant out to a $\frac{1}{4}$-inch (6 mm) thickness. The fondant will absorb cornstarch; as you're rolling, keep lifting the fondant and sprinkling cornstarch on the work surface to compensate. Also sprinkle the top surface of fondant, as needed. The diameter of the fondant should end

up equaling the measurement of the top of the cake plus both sides, with an extra couple of inches leeway.

3. Slip your hand under the fondant. Put it on top of the cake and smooth it down the sides.

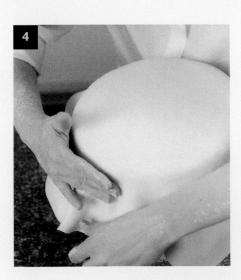

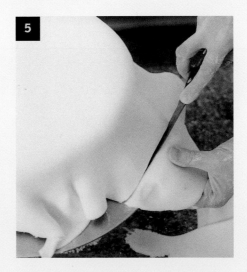

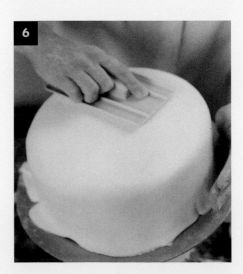

4. Gently press the fondant onto the cake, smoothing it with your hands as you do so. The sides will tend to bunch, so you should compensate by coaxing the fondant gently away from the cake, then smoothing it with your hand.

5. Roughly trim the excess fondant from the bottom edge of the cake with a sharp, straight-edged knife. If anything, err on the side of caution—leave too much. If you trim it too severely, making the border too short, there's no going back.

6. Do your final smoothing with an icing smoother. When you're done, do a clean trim around the bottom edge of cake, but make sure the entire side, including where it meets the cake board, remains covered in fondant.

TIPS

◆ Before applying the fondant, cover the cake with a thin layer of icing, called a crumb coat, or ganache to act as a glue to adhere the fondant to the surface of the cake.

◆ Once you've rolled out the fondant, you need to work relatively quickly, otherwise it will begin to dry out and the surface will harden and wrinkle. The entire process from rolling it out to covering a cake should take about five minutes.

◆ If you're going to emboss a quilted design on your cake, you need to do it soon after the cake is covered. You have a window of about an hour to work in, although it's best to do it immediately.

◆ Fondant is extremely sensitive to temperature. If it's too warm, the fondant will buckle, so you need to work in a cool room. If it's hot and humid outside, find yourself an air-conditioned space to work with the fondant and to store the cake in.

◆ Do not refrigerate or freeze fondant. It will get sticky and unusable.

◆ Too much cornstarch will dry out the fondant and may cause the surface to look cracked. Practice handling a fondant before covering a cake for the first time.

◆ After a cake is covered in fondant, it cannot be refrigerated, because the fondant will become tacky. However, the fondant will keep a cake fresh for several days by sealing it. (Once the cake has been cut, it's fine to refrigerate leftovers, although the fondant will get sticky.)

◆ Remove any rings or jewelry that may leave an impression in the fondant. It's best to wear a clean, light-colored apron so that clothing fibers or lint do not end up in the fondant.

QUILTING FONDANT

What you'll need: 1-inch- (2.5 cm) wide metal ruler, fondant-covered tier, tracing wheel, triangle

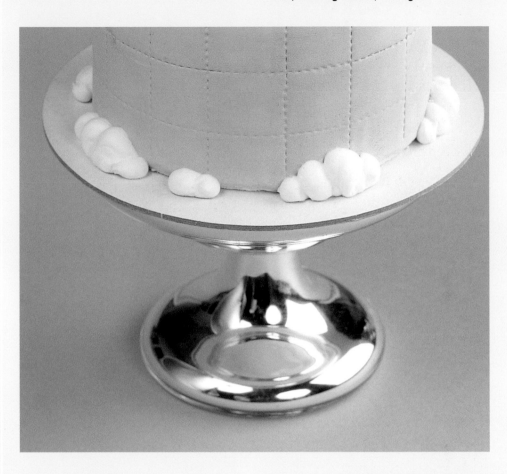

FOR THE TOP OF THE CAKE:

1. Place a 1-inch- (2.5 cm) wide metal ruler diagonally on top of the cake.

2. Run the tracing wheel along the edge of the ruler to mark a dotted line across the top of the fondant. Run the tracing wheel along the other side of the ruler. Use these lines as guides and continue marking diagonal lines in the same direction across the top of cake.

3. Use these lines as guides to mark lines crossing in the other direction.

FOR THE SIDES OF THE CAKE:

To make the vertical lines for a checkered pattern along the side of the cake, align the bottom edge of the triangle with the bottom edge of the cake and mark equidistant lines along the vertical edge of the triangle.

For horizontal lines of a checkered pattern, run the tracing wheel along the edge of the ruler moving the ruler along with the tracing wheel as you work your way around the cake.

For a diamond pattern, line up the bottom of the triangle with the bottom of the cake and score the dotted lines along the angled edge of the triangle.

25

Building a Tiered Cake

What you'll need: Bench scraper, fondant-covered tiers with the bottom tier already on its base (see Covering with Fondant, page 24), straws, food-color marker, scissors, royal icing, metal spatula

TIPS

◆ When you're building a cake, it gets surprisingly heavy very quickly. That's why we use straws as supports between the tiers to give the cake structure. Each tier has its own cake board, the upper tiers resting on the straws or dowels underneath. This holds up the tiers and keeps the cake from collapsing.

◆ The base that the bottom tier rests on must be strong enough to support the weight of all the tiers. I often like to use a ½-inch- (13 mm) thick premade foil-covered foam-core base because it's lightweight and strong. If you like, the base can be covered in fondant or a layer of thinned royal icing. It must then set for 24 hours.

◆ The fondant must be completely set before the tiers are stacked.

1. Use a bench scraper to clear off all residue from the work space.

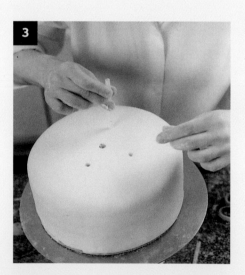

2. Place a straw in the center of tier to measure its height. Mark the place where you want to cut it with a food-color marker. (You can also use a regular marker, but make sure it doesn't touch the surface of the cake itself.) Remove the straw, and cut to size. Use this as a guide for the rest of the straws in that tier, and cut them to the same size.

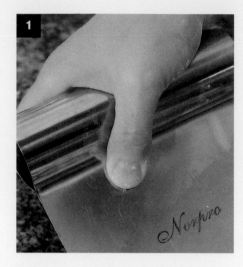

3. Place a straw back into the center of the tier. Place four more straws in a ring around the center straw, each halfway between the edge and the center. (For larger tiers, cut and place six more dowels.) Make sure each straw goes in straight; it's easy to stick them in crooked, but that will compromise the structure of the cake. Repeat steps 2 and 3 for all but the top tier of the cake.

4. Start assembling your tiers. Dot each bottom tier with royal icing to serve as glue. Center the next tier on top of it. When you're placing a tier, hold it underneath for support, and use the metal spatula for placement. Once you've got it placed, gently slide out your hand, then slide out the spatula.

5. Once the tier is in place, gently use your hands to make sure it's absolutely centered and level.

Transporting a Tiered Cake

When delivering a tiered cake to an event, I don't assemble it in advance. Instead, I bring each tier in a separate sturdy box and assemble it on site. I fasten the cake board to the box with just a few dots of hot glue or royal icing (make sure icing has time to set). Use enough so that it doesn't shift while in transit, but not so much that the cake won't come free when you arrive.

Cake equipment suppliers sell reinforced boxes for transporting tiers. They've got collapsible sides, to make it easier to get the cake into and out of the box. If you're using a standard cardboard box, just make sure that the bottom is very secure, and that you can just cut open the sides when you're ready to take out the cake. Bring along a long-bladed knife or spatula to slip under the cake board before you lift it from the box. Once I'm at the location, I stack and attach the tiers, and pipe all the bottom borders to finish off the cake.

Fragile three-dimensional decorations, such as gum-paste butterflies, can break easily in transit. I package them separately and put them on last. I always get to the location anywhere from 45 minutes to several hours early to allow enough time to assemble the cake and add the finishing details.

Filling an Icing Bag

What you'll need: Icing bag, coupler, decorating tip, tall glass, icing (pages 126–127), rubber spatula, paper towels

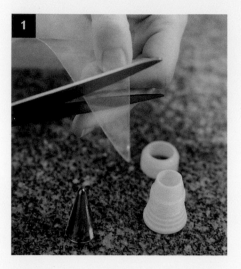

1. Snip off the triangular tip of the bag.

2. Place the larger piece of the coupler inside the bag, narrow end out. Put the decorating tip on top of that, then screw on the coupler ring.

3. Put the bag tip-down into a tall glass, then fold the excess plastic around the outside of the glass. Fill the bag with icing using the rubber spatula, using the rim of the glass to scrape the icing into the bag. Don't fill the icing bag more than halfway.

4. Lift the bag off the glass. Gather the bag just above the icing, then use the other hand to massage the icing downward, squeezing out any air bubbles.

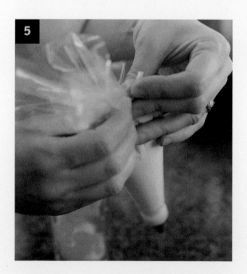

5. Hold the top of the bag closed (or use a twist tie) to maintain pressure as you squeeze the icing out.

TIPS

◆ I use a 10-inch (23 cm) plastic bag instead of the traditional cloth variety because of its ease of use and cleanup.

◆ While you're filling the bag, cover the mixing bowl with a damp cloth to keep the royal icing from drying out.

◆ Wad a moist paper towel in the bottom of the tall glass and set the icing bag tip-down in the glass while not in use. This keeps the icing at the end of the tip from hardening.

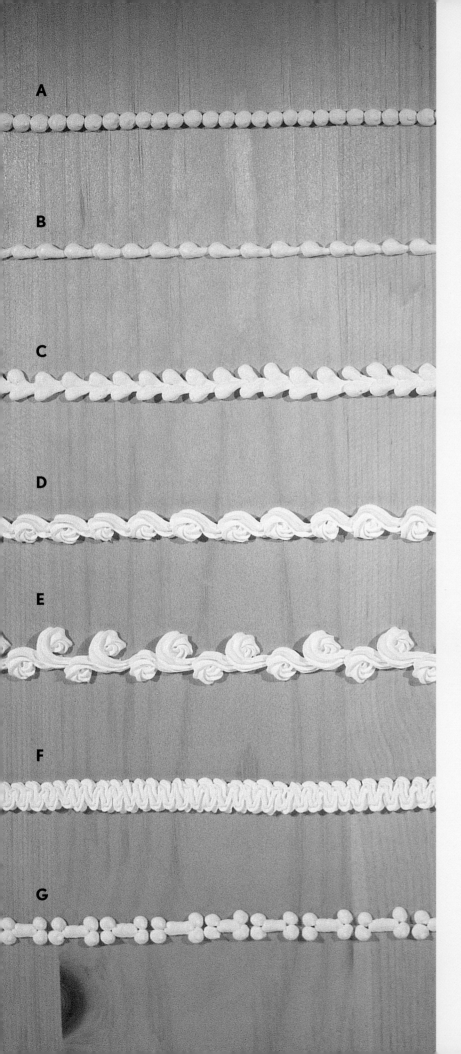

A

B

C

D

E

F

G

Piping Techniques

What you'll need: Filled icing bag

BORDERS

A | Beads

Use a round decorator tip. Hold the bag close to perpendicular. Apply steady pressure until you get the size bead you want. Ease off on the pressure, then pull the bag gently away to avoid forming a peak. Repeat until you've beaded the circumference of the cake.

B | Snail Trail

Use a round tip. Hold the bag at a 45-degree angle. Make a bulb of icing, then ease off pressure as you move sideways to create a trail, starting each bulb at the very end of the last one.

C | Hearts

This is just like a snail trail, except after piping each tear-shaped bulb, you pipe another one just below. Together, they form a heart shape.

D | Shells

Use a star tip. Hold the bag at a 45-degree angle. Apply even pressure, making a spiral and lifting the tip away from the surface to form the back of the shell. Ease up on the pressure and drag the tip down to form a point.

E | Reverse Shells

These are the same as shells, except instead of all rising up, you alternate having one shell faceup and the next one facedown.

F | Zigzag

Using a star tip, hold the bag at a 45-degree angle. Applying steady pressure, move the tip in a back and forth motion.

G | Dog Bones

This is not a standard border pattern, but something I made up for the Good Blue Dog Cake (page 55). Using a round tip, pipe two dots of icing, one directly above the other. Next, pipe a horizontal line or dash from the center of the two dots to form the long part of the bone. Pipe two more dots connected to the dash to finish it off.

29

BASKET WEAVE

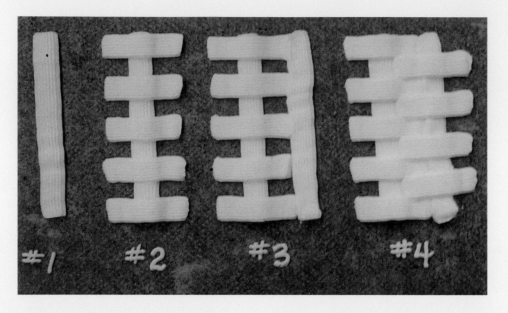

TIPS

◆ Piping techniques require a certain amount of finesse. It's a good idea to practice on a sheet of wax paper before using these on the cake itself.

◆ There are dozens of decorating tips in different shapes and sizes. Once you've gotten the basics down, mix and match techniques and make up your own patterns.

1. Using a basket-weave tip, hold the bag at a nearly perpendicular angle, with the tip tooth-side up. Make a straight, vertical strip along the side of the cake.

2. Pipe a series of short horizontal strips, each about 1 inch (2.5 cm) long, centered across the vertical strip. The space between the strips should be just big enough to pipe a strip in the opposite direction—in other words, the width of the tip.

3. Pipe another vertical line along one end of the horizontal strips.

4. Pipe another row of horizontal strips over the new vertical strip, filling in the spaces you've left open in the previous set of horizontal strips. Continue until you've covered the surface.

Tiny Roses

TOOLS:

Small flower nail, wax paper

1. Before you create the individual roses, you must create the cones that will serve as centers in advance. Tape the sides of a sheet of wax paper to the work surface. (This will keep it from lifting up while you're working. Using a #9 tip, pipe small cones on the wax paper, about $\frac{1}{2}$ inch (13 mm) tall. Pipe as many cones as you want roses. Let them dry completely.

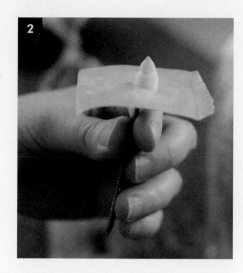

2. Cut another piece of wax paper into $1\frac{1}{2}$-inch (4 cm) squares. Affix a square to the flower nail with a tiny dab of icing. Take a cone, and stick that on the wax paper, centered on the flower nail, using another dab of icing.

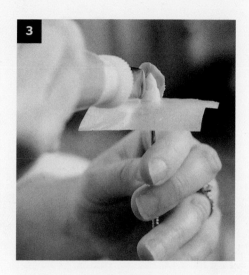

3. Use a #104 petal tip, sitting it on the flower nail surface with the wider end down, apply pressure evenly, and turn the nail as you squeeze out icing for 360° to form a bud.

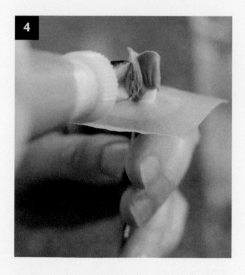

4. Continue piping petals around the bud.

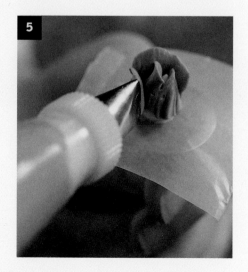

5. Pipe a total of three petals around the bud.

6. Make four or five petals to form the outer layer of the rose.

Chrysanthemums

ADDITIONAL TOOLS: *Large flower nail, wax paper*

1. Cut wax paper into $1\frac{1}{2}$-inch (4 cm) squares. Affix to a large flower nail with a tiny dab of icing. Using a #80 or #81 petal tip, keep the round part of the tip down: the tip should look like a smile, not a frown. Start halfway between the center and the edge of the nail, and pipe petals outward. When you get to the edge, just as you're about to ease up on the pressure, lift the tip upward to create a rim on the petal.

2. Continue piping a row of petals around the circumference.

3. Pipe a second row on top of the first row. Start each petal a little closer to the center, and end it a little farther from the edge.

4. Do a third row, closer still to the center, this time making shorter petals.

5. Finish the chrysanthemum with three or four small petals in the center.

FLOODING WITH THINNED ROYAL ICING

First pipe an outline of stiff royal icing, using a #2–#5 round decorating tip. Make a thinner royal icing to fill in the border by gradually adding a few drops of water until the icing has a syrupy consistency (page 127). Use a #3 tip held about $\frac{1}{2}$ inch (13 mm) above the surface to flood the outlines or you can use a spoon to apply the icing.

TIPS

◆ To test consistency, let a teaspoon of the thinned icing fall back into the bowl; it should disappear into the mix in about ten seconds.

◆ While the icing is still wet, you can even it out and fill in any gaps by dragging a toothpick through thinned icing, working it into place.

◆ Decorations flooded with royal icing should set for twenty-four hours.

◆ Wax paper is an indispensable tool when making any kind of removable free-standing royal icing decorations. The decorations are piped onto the wax paper, which can be peeled off once the decorations have dried.

Gum-Paste Decorations

What you'll need:
(See recipe on page 129) Gum-paste cutout or molded shapes, paper towel (Each cake with gum-paste decorations has specific instructions for cutting shapes.)

TIPS

◆ Heat and humidity can make your gum-paste decorations wilt or even melt, so be sure to make and store them in a cool place.

◆ Gum paste should always be kept covered to prevent it from drying out.

◆ To make gum-paste decorations stick to each other or to fondant, brush them with just a few drops of water, being careful not to make them wet and mushy. You can also make edible glue by mixing a small amount of gum paste and water.

◆ Gum-paste decorations can be kept indefinitely. (My mom has saved every gum-paste flower I've ever made for her—some are ten years old.) Gum paste dries to a hard porcelain-like finish.

◆ Dried decorations are fragile. Although they're hard, they're brittle, so they must be handled with care. Always make extra gum-paste decorations to allow for breakage.

◆ I don't recommend using ready-made gum paste. It's generally too soft to hold its shape well.

◆ For shaping blossoms and calyxes, use a ball tool to press into the flower and create a rounded shape.

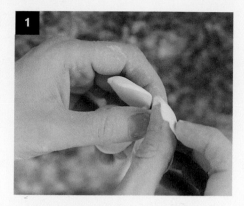

1. To shape a petal, use your thumb to mold it into the palm of your hand. Squeeze the edge between your thumb and forefinger to thin it out, getting rid of its mechanical, cookie-cutter look.

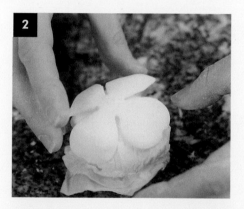

2. To dry a curved gum-paste decoration, wad up a small piece of paper towel to the size and shape of the curve you want, and let the object dry facedown on top.

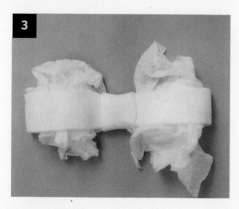

3. For a bow, place a small piece of crumpled paper towel or tissue inside each loop. When the bow is dry, remove.

33

Marzipan Decorations

What you'll need: (See recipe on page 129) Marzipan molded into figures or fruit, veining tool or toothpick (Each cake with marzipan decorations has detailed instructions for molding shapes.)

1. As you work the surface of a marzipan figure, the surface can begin to look cracked. This can be smoothed out by rubbing it with a little bit of water. Don't worry if the end result isn't perfectly smooth, since little imperfections become barely noticeable in the final product.

2. When shaping marzipan fruit, roll it into a ball, then use veining tools to create the little hollow space where the stem will go.

TIPS

◆ Try not to overwork marzipan. The oil from the almonds will start to surface, making it greasy.

◆ Brushing a few drops of water on a small area makes the marzipan tacky, letting you attach limbs to characters.

◆ If a piece of your molded figure is particularly heavy, you can insert a toothpick into the body, put a few drops of water on the surface, and stick the attachment on top. (Just remember to let your guests know that the toothpick's in there!)

◆ Marzipan will settle a little bit when you stack the pieces together. I usually compensate for this by making the bottom shapes just a little bit longer than I want, and also by propping pieces up while they're setting.

◆ Store-bought marzipan tastes great and works wonderfully.

Painting with Food Color

BRUSH PAINTING

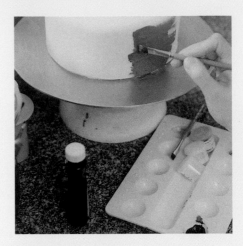

Mix 3 parts food color with 1 part lemon extract, adjusting to achieve a consistency halfway between watercolor paint and syrup. It should spread easily without streaking and be opaque enough to mask the fondant or royal icing. Paint the cake with smooth, even strokes.

TIPS

◆ Before you start, the icing must be completely set. Touch the cake lightly: the icing should be firm.

◆ Don't backtrack: painting over areas you've just painted will cause major streaks. If you want to redo a section, wait until it is thoroughly dry.

◆ The names I use for food colors in the cake instructions are descriptive of the color. I don't list any specific color names because the names vary from one manufacturer to another.

34

What you'll need:
Paintbrushes or sponges, palette or bowls for paint, powdered food color, lemon extract

◆ Before sponge painting on the cake itself, I recommend practicing on a rolled-out scrap of fondant or gum paste to see what effect you'll get.

◆ The fondant should be completely set before sponge painting.

◆ Don't apply a second coat until the first is completely dry.

SPONGE PAINTING

1. Mix food color and lemon extract. The mixture should be more viscous than for brush painting—almost syrupy. Dip the end of the sponge in food color.

2. Don't saturate the sponge, because you want to grab hold of the other end. Touch tip of sponge against the cake.

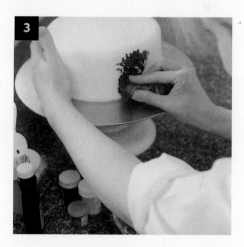

3. Continue dipping and dabbing until the cake is painted with a beautiful mottled effect.

Using Templates

What you'll need: Straight pins or fine-line food-color markers

TIPS

◆ You can use the templates I've provided at the end of the book, buy templates at a crafts store, or design your own.

◆ If you're using mine, you can either photocopy them or trace them onto tracing or parchment paper.

TEMPLATE

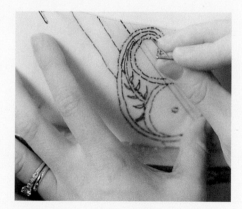

Cut the template to fit the side of the cake. Pin all four corners to hold it in place. Take your straight pin and mark holes, transferring the template design onto the cake by making pinholes. Remove the paper, and you have a guideline for piping your design.

STENCIL

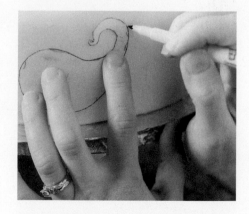

An alternative method: With a repeated pattern, cut out the main shape and use it as a stencil, tracing along the outside with a fine-line food-color marker.

35

Sculpted Figure Cakes

Sculpted figure confections can be

made out of a number of different edible claylike sugar pastes, but
I've been making them exclusively out of marzipan for years. I like the
substantial texture of marzipan and when it finally comes time to eat
it—it makes a pretty tasty treat.

In this chapter, I've focused on smaller, usually single-tier cakes, for
the sake of concentrating on the figures themselves. But sculpted figures
work on larger cakes as well. You can make elegant, witty decorative
sculptures that would highlight the most sophisticated wedding or gala.
When determining the size of the top tier, take into consideration the
size of the figure you're planning to make.

When you plan this sort of cake topper, keep the scale of the entire
cake in mind. You want the figures to be the focal point without either
overwhelming the cake or getting lost on too big a cake.

If you've never made marzipan sculptures before, the Pom-Pom Luv
Birds cake (page 38) or the pears from the Nutty Squirrel cake (page 45)
are great places to start. They both have very basic shapes, which you can
build upon as you become more comfortable with the process.

One word of advice—before serving up the characters, know your
audience! Once at a children's birthday party, a little boy asked if he
could eat the bear at the top of the cake. I handed him one of the
ears…and a bunch of the other kids ran out of the room screaming!
Oops! Still, you never know. I've seen tiny tots eating marzipan animals
off the tops of cakes—biting off the heads first!

POM-POM LUV BIRDS

POM-POM BIRDS ARE BUILT A LITTLE LIKE SNOWMEN—BY STACKING A COUPLE OF
SPHERES ON TOP OF EACH OTHER—SO IT'S A GREAT BEGINNER'S CAKE. IF YOU'VE
NEVER DONE AN ICING BASKET WEAVE BEFORE, IT MAY SEEM A LITTLE DAUNTING,
BUT IT'S EASIER THAN IT LOOKS. FOLLOW THE BASIC INSTRUCTIONS (PAGE 30) AND
PRACTICE ON A PIECE OF PAPER A FEW TIMES FIRST. YOU'LL HAVE IT DOWN IN NO
TIME. EVEN IF YOU'RE A MORE EXPERIENCED CAKE MAKER, IT'S A LOVELY LITTLE
MINIMALIST CAKE FOR ENGAGEMENTS, SHOWERS, OR BIRTHDAYS.

CAKE

- 5-inch (13 cm) round tier, 3 inches (8 cm) high

DECORATIONS

- Marzipan: 2 birds
- Gum paste: 4 berries, 4 leaves
- Powdered food color: black, buttercup yellow, and pink petal dust
- Paste food color: yellow, moss green, brown, and red
- Lemon extract
- Confectioners' sugar (for coating work surface)
- Buttercream icing (page 126)
- Royal icing (page 127)
- 1 teaspoon red nonpareils
- Cloth-covered wire: four green #24 gauge, 4 inches (10 cm) long
- Floral tape

EQUIPMENT

- 5-inch (13 cm) cake board
- Cake stand (optional)
- Icing tips: #5 round, #47 basket weave, #65 leaf
- Icing bag and coupler
- Craft paintbrushes
- Cutters: lily cutter (for leaves), small calyx
- Ball tool
- Wax paper
- Turntable
- Electric mixer
- Bench scraper

TECHNIQUES YOU'LL USE

Slicing, filling, and coating a cake
(page 22)

Piping techniques
(page 29)

Marzipan decorations
(page 34)

Painting with food color
(page 34)

TIMING TIPS

Depending on the weather, the smooth coating of royal icing on the top of the cake will take between twelve and twenty-four hours to set completely, so it's best to bake this cake at least two days in advance and apply the top coating at least a day before. (If the top coat of icing isn't set, the weight of the marzipan may make it crack.) The marzipan decorations can be made up to two weeks in advance and kept in airtight containers.

SCULPTED FIGURE CAKES

IN ADVANCE

1 **Make the marzipan birds** (see A, B, and C, page 40). Start by kneading yellow food color paste into about three-quarters of the marzipan, a few drops at a time. **2** Work moss green food coloring into a little bit of the gum paste, and add a slight touch of brown to mute the color. Roll out the paste very thin with a small rolling pin and use leaf cutters to cut out four leaves. (Reserve some of the green gum paste for the calyxes of the berries.) Let dry on a crumpled piece of paper towel (to create curve) overnight. **3** Make four gum-paste and nonpareil berries (see D, page 40). **4** Paint the birds' beaks with buttercup yellow petal dust and lemon extract and the birds' tails with pink. Paint black dots to make eyes.

5. Bake and cool the cake completely.

6. Attach the cake to cake board, and chill, fill, and apply crumb coat to the sides of the cake only. (The buttercream will break down the royal icing used to form the smooth surface on top of the cake.)

7. Place the cake on a cake stand and secure with royal icing.

8. **Pipe basket-weave pattern**, using the #47 basket-weave decorating tip, around the outside of the cake (see page 30). Mix a small amount of moss green paste food coloring into buttercream icing, and add a slight touch of brown to mute the color a bit.

9. Cover the top of the cake with a smooth layer of royal icing. Create a beaded royal icing outline around the top edge of the cake using the #5 round decorating tip. Flood the outline border with thinned royal icing to cover the top of the cake (see page 33). Let it harden completely.

10. With the #5 round decorating tip, pipe royal icing hearts onto the border, spaced one at the top of every other vertical line of basket weave. When dry, paint the hearts pink.

11. **Attach the birds** to the completely hardened top of the cake with a few dabs of royal icing. Attach leaves and berries to cake.

DECORATING DETAILS

A | MOLD THE MARZIPAN

Roll two balls of marzipan, an approximately 2-inch (5 cm) diameter body and a $1\frac{1}{2}$-inch (4 cm) diameter head. Starting with a pea-sized ball, mold a cone beak. Using a rolling pin, roll a tail about $\frac{1}{16}$-inch (1.5 mm) thick, 3 inches long (8 cm), and $\frac{1}{2}$-inch (2 cm) wide; then cut a triangle from the end. Dry on an icing tip to create a curve.

B | ATTACH TAIL AND BEAK

Stick the tail to the bottom of the larger ball with a drop of water. Attach the beak to the head with water. Place a toothpick into the larger ball as a support for stacking the head.

C | COMPLETE THE BIRD

Brush a few drops of water around the toothpick and place the head on top of body. Let set overnight. When making the second bird, position the head so that it will nuzzle the first bird.

D | MAKE THE GUM PASTE BERRIES

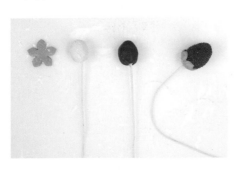

Roll a small oval of gum paste. Roll out the green gum paste very thin and use small calyx cutters to cut out four calyxes. Gently press a ball tool into the calyx to give petals curved shape. Make a small hook at end of a medium-gauge wire wrapped in florist tape, moisten, and insert into oval. Thin a small amount of red royal icing and brush onto surface. Dip the icing covered oval into red nonpareils, let dry. Place calyx onto wire and attach to berry with water.

ELLA FANT DANCE

THIS MINIATURE CIRCUS ELEPHANT IS PRACTICING HER BALANCING ACT. THIS IS
A GREAT CAKE FOR KIDS. MY NIECE AND NEPHEW KATE AND ZACH GUARDED THE
LITTLE MARZIPAN ELEPHANT LIKE A PRECIOUS TREASURE, BUT THEY WERE ALSO
FASCINATED BY THE IDEA THAT THEY COULD EAT IT...IF THEY WANTED TO.

CAKES

- 2 halves of 6-inch (15 cm) ball cakes

DECORATIONS

- Marzipan: elephant
- Powdered food color: yellow, moss green, royal blue, deep orange, red, gray, and white
- Lemon extract
- Royal icing (page 127)
- Cornstarch (for coating fondant work surface)
- Confectioners' sugar (for coating marzipan work surface)
- Food-color marker: fine-line black
- Fondant (page 128)

EQUIPMENT

- Cake boards: 6-inch (15 cm) round boards
- Cake stand (optional) or 8-inch (20 cm) foam-core base
- Icing tip: #4 round
- Icing bag and coupler
- Cookie cutter: 2-inch (5 cm) circle
- Craft paintbrushes
- Toothpicks
- Ruler
- Rolling pin
- Metal spatula
- Electric mixer
- Bench scraper
- Icing smoother

TECHNIQUES YOU'LL USE

Slicing, filling, and coating a cake (page 22)

Covering with fondant (page 24)

Piping techniques; borders (page 29)

Marzipan decorations (page 34)

Painting with food color (page 34)

TIMING TIPS

The marzipan elephant can be made anytime from one day to two weeks ahead of time and kept in an airtight container. Bake the cake two days in advance. Since the unique shape of the cake needs to be extra sturdy, you want time for it to become well chilled, and for the filling and then the fondant to set completely.

IN ADVANCE

• • •

1 Make the marzipan elephant (see A and B, below). Let dry overnight so that the limbs, head, and ears are set in place. **2** Paint the tusks and toenails with white powdered food color and lemon extract. Paint the rest of the elephant gray (see B, below). Blend a mixture of gray powdered food color and lemon extract. If you'd like to mix your own gray color, start with 5 parts white and add 1 part black powdered color. Add more black or white to get the exact shade you'd like. **3** Use a black fine-line food-color marker or a fine-detail paintbrush to add the eyes and outlines to the tusks, feet, trunk, and toenails.

4. Bake and cool cake completely.

5. **To make a ball-shaped cake,** set, but do not attach, the half-sphere cakes onto cake boards for easier handling and chill well.

6. Place first half, rounded-side down, on a cake board. Cover the flat top with buttercream for filling and stack second half circle flat-side down on top of it to form ball (see C, below). Chill the cake.

7. Place the ball-shaped cake on a cake stand or base and secure with icing.

8. Cover with a thin layer of buttercream icing.

9. Cover with fondant.

10. **Make guidelines for coloring cake sections.** Start with the small circle that the elephant will stand on at the top of the ball. Use a 2-inch (5 cm) circle cookie cutter to make a light impression on top of the cake to mark the circle.

11. Use a toothpick to trace along the side of a piece of paper or a ruler to make guidelines dividing the cake in half. Next, divide each half section into thirds to create six sections for the six different colors on the ball. Let fondant set.

12. Paint five of the sections with powdered food color mixed with lemon extract. The sixth section will be left white. The colors on the cake shown are: royal blue, yellow, moss green, orange, white, and red (in that order). You can choose your own colors to match the color scheme of your party.

13. **Pipe the royal icing outlines** over the guidelines that divide the cake into sections of different colors and the little circle on top using the #4 tip.

14. Place Ella on top of the cake. Insert two toothpicks into two of the legs (not raised front leg), to help her balance.

DECORATING DETAILS

• • •

A | SHAPE THE MARZIPAN

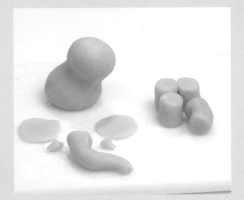

FOR HEAD AND BODY: a bottom-heavy peanutlike shape.
EARS: flat discs.
TUSKS: little horn shapes.
TRUNK: like a tapered teapot spout.
LEGS: short Tootsie Rolls.

B | COMPLETE THE ELEPHANT

Dab a few drops of water on tops of the three legs to support elephant. Set the body on top with the head pointing upward. Hold in place until it feels steady. Attach ears, then the trunk and tusks. Last, secure the lifted front leg. Use small pieces of wadded paper towel as supports while drying.

C | FILL CAKE BEFORE ICING

43

NUTTY SQUIRREL

I LOVE THE ELEMENT OF PLAYFULNESS THAT THE NUTTY SQUIRREL BRINGS TO THIS CAKE, BUT IF YOU DON'T FEEL READY TO MAKE SCULPTED CHARACTERS, BY ALL MEANS MAKE JUST THE FRUIT AND ACORNS. IT'S A GREAT AUTUMNAL CAKE EITHER WAY. THE FIRST TIME I MADE MARZIPAN FRUIT AND NUTS, I WAS IMPRESSED BY HOW BASIC THE SHAPES ARE. WITH VERY LITTLE SKILL OR EFFORT, A BALL OF MARZIPAN AND SOME FOOD COLOR CAN BE TRANSFORMED INTO A VERY REALISTIC PEAR.

TIMING TIPS
▪ ▪ ▪

The marzipan decorations can be made anywhere from one day to two weeks ahead of time and kept in an airtight container. Since most of the decorations are made in advance, once the cake has been covered in fondant, the rest shouldn't take much time at all.

CAKE

- 8-inch (20 cm) round cake

DECORATIONS

- Marzipan: 4 pears, 6 acorns, and 1 squirrel
- 10 cloves (for stems)
- Powdered food color: yellow, moss green, brown, deep orange, black, and white
- Paste food color: sky blue
- Lemon extract
- Royal icing (page 127)
- Black jellybean (for eyes)
- Sprinkles: ivory (or chocolate)
- Fondant (page 128)
- Cornstarch (for coating fondant work surface)
- Confectioners' sugar (for coating marzipan work surface)

EQUIPMENT

- Cake board: 8-inch (20 cm) round board
- Cake stand (optional) or 10-inch (25 cm) foam-core base
- Craft paintbrushes
- Flower tools: veining, ball
- Small, sharp straight-edge knife
- Toothpicks
- Rolling pin
- Metal spatula
- Turntable
- Electric mixer
- Bench scraper
- Icing smoother

TECHNIQUES YOU'LL USE
▪ ▪ ▪

Slicing, filling, and coating a cake (page 22)

▪ ▪ ▪

Covering with fondant (page 24)

▪ ▪ ▪

Marzipan decorations (page 34)

▪ ▪ ▪

Painting with food color (page 34)

IN ADVANCE

■ ■ ■

1 Make the marzipan squirrel, fruit, and nuts. Mold the squirrel (see A and B, opposite). Form the pears (see C, opposite) and acorns (see D, opposite). Let dry. **2** To make the eyes, use a small, sharp straight-edge knife to cut both tips off of a black jelly-bean. When you cut them they form little points on the sides due to the pressure of the knife. You can emphasize this shape by squeezing the points between your thumb and forefinger to make the corner shapes of an eye. **3 Paint the marzipan sculptures.** For the squirrel: just before you are ready to use each color, mix the powdered food colors with lemon extract to form opaque paints the consistency of milk. Start with white for the inside of the legs, stomach, chest, ears, muzzle, and around eyes. Next, use light brown for the rest of the head and body. Add a darker brown stripe, starting above the nose and running behind the ears and down the back and tail. Paint a tiny black heart-shaped nose. **4 Give Nutty a bushy tail.** Thin a small amount of royal icing to the consistency of thick syrup. Brush the icing onto the back of the tail to act as edible glue. While it's wet, coat it with a thick layer of sprinkles. Let dry. **5** Paint acorns. Make the caps brown and the nut green. **6** Color pears. The colors are dusted directly onto the fruit with a dry brush (without using lemon extract). Start by covering a pear in either yellow or green powdered color and then lightly touch the surface with red or brown to create blushes on curves or indents. Blend smoothly from dark areas to lighter with touches of reds and browns.

7. Bake and cool cake completely.

8. Attach the cake to its board. Chill, fill, and apply crumb coat.

9. Knead blue food-color paste into fondant. Cover the cake with fondant. Let set.

10. Place on cake stand or base and secure with icing.

11. Paint the sides of the cake in smooth, even strokes. Combine 4 parts orange, 1 part red, and $\frac{1}{2}$ part brown powdered food color to create a deep rusty orange. Mix color with lemon extract. Once it's dry, you can give it another coat to make the color opaque.

12. Use toothpicks to attach a line of four acorns to the front of the cake.

13. Center Nutty the squirrel on top of the cake, and arrange the pears and remaining two acorns around him.

A | SHAPE THE MARZIPAN SQUIRREL

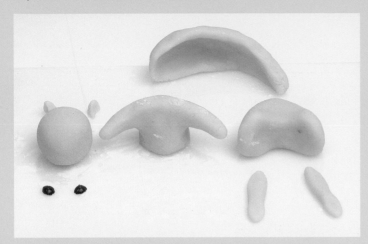

FOR HEAD: a ball with the front slightly tapered for nose.

EARS: form two small semicircles, hollow out center, and form nearly pointed tips.

UPPER BODY: start with a ball slightly larger than head, flatten bottom. Pull up and outward to form an arc for arms, keeping a rounded tummy.

LOWER BODY: Form a triangle slightly larger than upper body. Use thumbs to smooth curved shape for inner haunches.

LEGS: narrow tubes with indents for ankles.

TAIL: curved spoon shape tapered at the end.

B | COMPLETE THE SQUIRREL

Using small dabs of water, set lower body on top of legs with feet sticking out in front. Attach upper body. Use a toothpick to attach head. The tail will not be attached until just before placing on cake. Set ears and eyes in place on head.

C | SHAPE THE PEARS

Start with a golf-ball-sized piece of marzipan and a clove. Form pear shape. Use veining tool to indent stem area. Remove bottom of clove, leaving just a stem. Insert into pear. Insert bottom pointed cap of clove into bottom of pear.

D | SHAPE THE ACORNS

Start with one pea-sized and one grape-sized ball of marzipan. Form cap by hollowing smaller one with ball tool. Press side of toothpick against cap to make diagonal lines for texture. Repeat in other direction to create crosshatch pattern. Form little point on tip of larger ball. Attach cap to nut. Insert a clove for the stem.

BLUE BIRDS

CARTOONS FROM THE 1930S INSPIRED THIS CAKE, WHICH HAS A LITTLE FUN WITH SOME OLD-FASHIONED MARITAL CLICHÉS. MARZIPAN BIRDS SIT LOVE-STRUCK INSIDE AN IDYLLIC WHITE PICKET FENCE—BUT...THE GROOM SPORTS A BALL AND CHAIN. IT'S A REFERENCE TO MY HUSBAND'S HENNY YOUNGMAN ATTITUDE TOWARD CONNUBIAL BLISS. NOT MINE, THOUGH— THE BRIDE'S VERSION OF THE CAKE IS CIRCLED BY HEARTS, FLOWERS, AND PUFFS OF FROSTING CLOUDS.

CAKE

- 4-inch (10 cm) round tier, 3 (8 cm) inches high
- 5-inch (13 cm) round tier, 3 (8 cm) inches high

DECORATIONS

- Marzipan: 2 birds, 2 large hearts, 1 small heart, and 1 ball
- Gum paste: 22 blossoms, 22 slats for fence, 4 bee wings, 2 bee bodies
- Paste food color: blue
- Powdered food color: sky blue, reddish orange, pink, black, yellow, and white petal dust; white sparkle luster dust
- Food-color marker: black fine-line (or the fine lines can be painted using a very fine brush and black food color)
- Lemon extract
- Cornstarch (for coating fondant and gum paste work surfaces)
- Confectioners' sugar (for coating marzipan work surface)
- Floral wire
- Crystal decorating sugar
- Royal icing (page 127)
- Fondant (page 128)

EQUIPMENT

- Cake board: 4 inches (10 cm); 5-inch (13 cm) separator boards
- Base: 7-inch (18 cm) press board
- Cake stand (optional)
- Icing tips: #2, #3, and #9 round
- Icing bags and couplers
- Cutters: blossom, $2\frac{1}{2}$-inch (6 cm) scalloped heart, and $1\frac{1}{2}$-inch (4 cm) heart
- Ball modeling tool
- 90-degree triangle
- Tracing wheel
- Craft paintbrushes
- Plastic straws
- Toothpicks
- Rolling pin
- Metal spatulas
- Wax paper
- Scissors
- Turntable
- Electric mixer
- Bench scraper
- Icing smoother

TECHNIQUES YOU'LL USE

• • •

Slicing, filling, and coating a cake (page 22)

• • •

Covering with fondant (page 24)

• • •

Building a tiered cake (page 26)

• • •

Piping techniques; borders (page 29)

• • •

Gum-paste decorations (page 33)

• • •

Marzipan decorations (page 34)

• • •

Painting with food color (page 34)

IN ADVANCE

■ ■ ■

1 Sculpt the marzipan birds (see A, B, and C, opposite). **2** Make the ball for the ball and chain by rolling a blueberry-sized ball of marzipan. **3** For hearts, roll marzipan to $\frac{1}{4}$-inch (6 mm) thickness and cut out with cookie cutters. Let dry. **4** Make the gum-paste bees (see D, opposite). **5** Make the gum-paste fence (see E, opposite). **6** Roll out a thin layer of gum paste and cut out twenty-two blossoms with the blossom cutter and give blossoms a concave shape with the ball tool. Make a few extra in case some break. Let dry overnight. **7 Paint birds, bees, and the ball** with powdered food color mixed with lemon extract. (Always start with white.) **8** For the birds, paint the whites of the eyes and wedding dress first, then the blue of the bodies. Next paint the buttercup yellow beaks and bottom of the groom's feet. Draw in the black details using a fine-line food-color marker or paint with a fine brush. **9** Paint the bees' wings and the edges and backs of hearts with white sparkle mixed with powdered food color and lemon extract. Paint their bodies bright yellow, then the black details of the stripes. Their smiley faces can be made with the food-color marker over the yellow. **10** Paint the little blossoms pink with orange boarders. **11 Coat the hearts with crystal decorating sugar.** Pipe an icing outline just inside the edge of the hearts. Flood the outline boarder with thinned royal icing. Sprinkle sugar on top. Let dry overnight before shaking off excess sugar. **12** Paint the surface of the Bee Mine heart with pink food color and an orange outline. **13** Use a #2 round decorating tip to pipe the words Bee Mine on the front of the heart, and when it's dry, paint them black.

14. Bake and cool cakes completely.

15. Attach to cake boards, chill, fill, and apply crumb coat.

16. Attach 5-inch (13 cm) tier to 7-inch (18 cm) base.

17. **Cover the bottom (larger) tier with blue fondant.** Knead a small amount of blue paste food color into the fondant and cover.

18. While the blue fondant is still soft, make a quilted pattern on the top and sides of the tier. Line up the triangle with the bottom of the tier and make vertical lines about 1 inch (2.5 cm) apart. Use the vertical lines as a guide in making the horizontal lines with the triangle or ruler. The lines should be spaced about 1 inch (2.5 cm) apart.

19. Cover the top tier with white fondant. Make a quilted pattern on just the top surface of the cake using the technique described above. Let both tiers set overnight.

20. Cut support straws to size and insert into the 5-inch (13 cm) tier.

21. Center and attach the 4-inch (10 cm) to the 5-inch (13 cm) tier with icing.

22. **Attach the white picket fence** to the 4-inch (10 cm) tier by brushing very small dots of water on the backs of the slats and then gently pressing for a few seconds onto fondant. Let set.

23. When the fence is secure, attach the blossoms to the fence. They should each be placed about 1 inch (2.5 cm) from the top of the fence, and in between every other slat, using a small dot of royal icing as glue. Pipe a dot of icing into the center of each flower with the #3 round decorating tip. When the icing is dry, paint the centers yellow.

24. Attach the bees and the small Bee Mine heart to front of the fence with royal icing.

25. **Pipe beads of royal icing** using the #3 round decorating tip to form swags between the blossoms. Pipe a little loop of beads next to one of the bees. Pipe beads along the bottom of the 4-inch (10 cm) tier at the space between the slats.

26. **Pipe puffs of clouds** at the base of the cake, using the #9 round decorating tip. Squeeze and hold the icing bag in place a little longer to form the fatter parts of the clouds.

27. Use royal icing to attach the birds and the ball on top of the cake. Add their wings with water so that they hug.

28. Affix the blossoms around them, and then the large hearts with a little bit of royal icing. Use a few toothpicks behind the hearts to support them.

29. Use the #3 round decorating tip to pipe dots to form a chain from the ball to the groom's ankle. When dry, paint the chain and little cuff on his ankle (the leg iron) black.

30. **Attach a blossom** to the top of the bride's head and pipe some little curls onto the couple's heads using the #3 round decorating tip.

A | **MOLD THE MARZIPAN BRIDE**

Roll two balls of marzipan, 1 ½ -inch (4 cm) round for the head and a slightly smaller one for the body. Form a pear shape from the smaller ball for body. Make two tiny round cheeks. Shape wings and legs. Make indents in legs for body to sit on. Bring toes to point and form tiny heels for shoes. Mold two triangles for beaks. Make tail with rolling pin. Cut 1 inch (2.5 cm) long, ¾ -inch (2 cm) wide. Cut triangle from end.

B | **MOLD THE MARZIPAN GROOM**

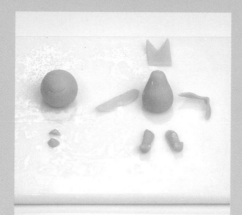

Roll two balls of marzipan, 1 ½ -inch (4 cm) round each. Form a pear shape from one for the body. Shape wings and legs. Make indents in legs for body to sit on. Form little V-shaped feet. Mold two triangles for beaks. Make tail with rolling pin. Cut 1 inch (2.5 cm) long, ¾ -inch (2 cm) wide. Cut triangle from end.

C | **COMPLETE THE BIRDS**

Cut toothpick about ½ inch (13 mm) shorter and insert into center of bodies as support. Place heads onto toothpicks. Secure the heads and legs to the bodies with water. Let set. Attach the wings after the birds are placed on top of the cake, so that they can touch each other.

D | **MOLD THE GUM-PASTE BEES**

Roll two jellybean shapes for bodies. For the bee's wings, take four tiny pieces of gum paste and squeeze between thumb and forefinger. Cut out four circles with the fat end of any of the icing tips.

E | **MAKE THE FENCE**

Roll out a thin layer of gum paste. Use a bench scraper, or other straight edge to cut strips measuring 3 ½ inches × ½ inch (9 cm × 13 mm). Cut triangle point in top ½ inch (13 mm) of strips.

Portrait Cakes

The first time I ever attempted any kind

of portrait on a cake, I'd gotten an assignment from the *New York Times* magazine to make a cake that looked like Martha Stewart (page 119). I was thrilled, but honestly had no clue how to go about it. Then I remembered a 1976 cake decoration book of mine, a kitsch classic in honor of the bicentennial. One of its highlights was a series of presidential portraits that looked to me like paint-by-numbers pictures. This gave me my inspiration. I broke down Martha's picture into small areas, each with its own color icing. When I got done decorating—well, there was Martha!

The "ice-by-numbers" approach, which I used for the Viva Elvis! cake (page 61), is probably the most complicated. So, I've started this chapter with a simple silhouette profile. It's an idea that dates back to the eighteenth century, when silhouettes were made by casting a shadow onto paper stretched between the subject and the artist. The concept may be old, but silhouettes can look very contemporary. Our Blue Dog portrait is done with a dog cookie cutter. It's fast and easy, but it still makes a hip, elegantly stylized statement.

You can also paint a portrait. This is an especially good option for the painter who wants to swap acrylics and canvas for buttercream and cake. The Baby Face Cake (page 65) is one idea, but the technique can be used for any portrait at all, from a simple cartoon face to a realistic likeness.

Nowadays, state-of-the-art technology has come to cake making. You can have photographs scanned onto edible paper with edible inks, or get a silkscreen made, which you then transfer onto your cake with cocoa powder. Both techniques are pretty amazing, and the results have a lot of eye appeal. But I still prefer the special look and feel of a handmade, one-of-a-kind product. And the honoree is always touched by the effort (although I have to admit—I never got Martha's reaction to her cake!).

GOOD BLUE DOG

WHEN YOU'VE GOT A DOG, YOU LOVE HIM OR HER ABSOLUTELY AND UNCONDITIONALLY. AT LEAST, THAT'S THE ATTITUDE OF MY DOG-OWNING FRIENDS, AND THAT'S WHY THIS CAKE INCLUDES A HALO AND GOLDEN DOG BONES. DEPENDING ON WHOM I SHOW IT TO, THIS IS A SILHOUETTE OF DIANA OR BAILEY OR TOAST OR BO. IT'S ALL DONE WITH SIMPLE COOKIE CUTTERS, WHICH YOU USE TO CUT OUT BROWN FONDANT SHAPES FROM THE CAKE, REPLACING THEM WITH BLUE FONDANT SHAPES. NOT ONLY DO I LIKE THE WAY THIS LOOKS, BUT IT'S A LOT OF PAYOFF FOR JUST A LITTLE EFFORT.

TIMING TIPS

• • •

The background brown color of the fondant was painted on because I like the contrast, matte finish, and texture of the brush strokes, but you can tint the fondant brown with paste food color or use chocolate fondant for the background. This is a fast and easy cake either way.

CAKE

- 7-inch (18 cm) round tier, 3 inches (8 cm) high

DECORATIONS

- Fondant
- Cornstarch (for coating fondant work surface)
- Paste food color: turquoise
- Powdered food color: brown petal dust, gold luster dust
- Lemon extract
- Royal icing (page 127)

EQUIPMENT

- Cake board: 7-inch (18 cm) round board
- Cake stand (optional) or 8-inch (20 cm) base
- Icing tips: #3 and #4 round
- Icing bag and coupler
- Cookie cutters: dog, dog bone, 1- and 2-inch (2.5 and 5 cm) circles
- Craft paintbrushes
- Toothpicks
- Rolling pin
- Metal spatula
- Electric mixer
- Bench scraper
- Icing smoother

TECHNIQUES YOU'LL USE

— • • • —

Slicing, filling, and coating a cake
(page 22)

• • •

Covering with fondant
(page 24)

• • •

Piping techniques
(page 29)

• • •

Painting with food color
(page 34)

1. Bake and cool cake completely.

2. Attach the cake to its board. Chill, fill, and apply crumb coat.

3. Cover the cake with fondant.

4. **Make the good dog cutouts.** Center the dog cookie cutter on top of the cake and press to cut out dog shape. Carefully lift out the fondant dog shape.

5. **Paint the background brown.** Use a wide, flat paintbrush and make broad strokes to paint the background of the cake with brown powdered food color mixed with lemon extract. Use a smaller brush at the edges.

6. **Make the blue dog.** Knead the turquoise paste food color into fondant (set aside a little bit of the blue fondant to make donut shapes for side of cake). Roll out the fondant and use the same dog cookie cutter to cut out a blue dog shape (see A, below). Inlay the blue dog into the open space left in the chocolate fondant and gently coax it into place so that the edges meet (see B, below).

7. Repeat this process to cut out the chocolate fondant dog bones from the side of the cake and replace with blue (or white) dog bones, which will be painted gold.

8. Use the icing smoother to even out the top and sides of the cake.

9. Paint the dog bones with gold luster dust mixed with lemon extract. Let dry (see C, below).

10. Cut out five 2-inch (5 cm) blue fondant circles. Cut a 1-inch (2.5 cm) hole just off center in the circles. Use a few drops of water to affix the donut shapes to sides of cake in a random pattern.

11. Pipe a small ring above the dog's head for a halo.

12. Scratch off little lines of brown color with a toothpick to make the rays around the halo.

13. **Pipe the borders.** Use the #4 round decorating tip to pipe dots around the top edge of the cake. Pipe a border of dog bones along bottom edge of the cake (see page 29).

DECORATING DETAILS

• • •

A | CUT OUT DOG SHAPES

Press dog cookie cutter into fondant on cake and remove dog. Use same cookie cutter to make blue dog.

B | BLUE DOG INLAY

Gently place the blue dog into fondant and coax into place so that the edges meet.

C | PAINT THE DOG BONES

Mix gold luster dust with lemon extract and paint bone cutouts using a medium round paintbrush, taking care to stay in the lines.

MONKEY FACE CAKE

I CAN'T HELP BUT SMILE WHEN I LOOK AT THIS HAPPY MONKEY FACE. AS I WRITE THIS BOOK, I'M PREGNANT WITH OUR FIRST CHILD. EVEN THOUGH THE BIRTH IS A COUPLE OF MONTHS OFF, SOMEHOW WE'VE ALREADY AMASSED A VERY COOL COLLECTION OF STUFFED ANIMALS, MOST OF THEM MONKEYS. I BAKED THIS CAKE IN HONOR OF OUR OWN SWEET LITTLE MONKEY-FACE-TO-BE.

TIMING TIPS

You'll want the ears to hold their shape when you attach them to the cake, so make them at least twenty-four hours in advance. The rest is fun and easy. The cake gets its basic shape from an oval pan. Follow the template for the face, and attach the ears with toothpicks.

CAKE

- 11-inch (28 cm) oval, 3 inches (8 cm) high

DECORATIONS

- Buttercream icing (page 126)
- Royal icing (page 127)
- Cornstarch (for coating fondant work surfaces)
- Paste food color: ivory, brown, blue, and orange
- Powdered food color: black, brown
- Lemon extract
- Fondant and gum-paste (page 128–129) ears
- Jellybeans: black, for eyes
- Ribbon: 2 yards of ½-inch (13 mm) rust or brown velvet ribbon

EQUIPMENT

- Cake boards: 11-inch (28 cm) round, trimmed to oval
- Base: 12-inch (30 cm) fondant-covered foam-core
- Decoration template for face (page 131)
- Icing tips: #4 round and #20 star
- Icing bags and couplers
- Craft paintbrushes
- Toothpicks
- Skewers
- Turntable
- Metal spatula
- Rolling pin
- Electric mixer
- Bench scraper
- Icing smoother
- Hot glue gun

TECHNIQUES YOU'LL USE

Slicing, filling, and coating a cake (page 22)

Covering with fondant (page 24)

Piping techniques (page 29)

Gum-paste decorations (page 33)

Painting with food color (page 34)

Using templates (page 35)

58

IN ADVANCE

· · ·

1 **Make the ears.** Combine equal parts of gum paste and fondant to make a pliable modeling paste that will dry to a firm but not brittle finish. To color, mix in a small amount of ivory paste food color. Shape the ears (see A and B, below). **2** Insert a toothpick halfway into the side of the ear that will be attached to the head. The extended end will act as a support to keep the ears in place. Let set for at least twenty-four hours. **3** Color the fondant that will be used to cover the cake with a small amount of ivory paste food color, kneading the fondant until the color is even. Seal in plastic and set aside. **4** **Prepare the cake base.** Color the fondant with a small amount of blue paste food color. Cover the 12-inch (30 cm) base with blue fondant. Let set for at least twenty-four hours. Attach $\frac{1}{2}$-inch (13 mm) ribbon to the edge of the fondant-covered base with a hot glue gun.

5. Bake and cool cake completely.

6. Attach the cake to its board. Chill, fill, and apply crumb coat.

7. Cover the cake with fondant. Let set.

8. Place on cake base and secure with icing.

9. Gently place the template on top of the cake. Pin all four corners in place. Transfer the template design onto the cake by making pinholes following the lines of the template. Remove the template, and you have a guideline for piping your design.

10. **Pipe the face.** Make the royal icing nose, mouth, and face outline using the #4 round decorating tip. Mix black food color with lemon extract and make the outline black using a fine-line paintbrush. Use the same technique to paint the nose and mouth brown.

11. Attach the jellybean eyes with a little bit of royal icing.

12. **Attach the ears.** First position the skewers as supports; measure about 2 inches (5 cm) from the base of the cake and halfway between the top of the head and the chin and score with a toothpick. Place two skewers level on either side of the head about 1 inch (2.5 cm) apart from each other. Guide an ear, toothpick-end first, along the skewers and slide into position, inserting the exposed toothpick into the cake.

13. **Pipe the fur** (see C, below). Mix the rust color by combining small amounts of orange and brown paste food color into the buttercream. Using the #20 star decorating tip, start piping a continuous row of stars around the outline of the face and then around the bottom edge of the cake that meets the base. Continue piping rows of stars around the face, working downward to the bottom of the cake until it is completely filled in. Pipe around the edges of the ears last.

DECORATING DETAILS

· · ·

A | SHAPE MONKEY EAR

Mold the modeling paste into a three-quarter moon. Begin to form a lip around the outer edge.

B | FINISH THE EAR

Use your thumbs to curve the edge of the ear. (To make the straight edge conform to fit monkey's head, press it gently against side of cool oval pan.)

C | PIPE THE FUR

Use the #20 star decorating tip to pipe rows of stars around the face and down the sides of the cake.

VIVA ELVIS!

WITH SO MANY ELVIS IMPERSONATORS OUT THERE, I FIGURED THAT IT WAS TIME FOR A CHOCOLATE-CAKE ELVIS TO HIT THE SCENE—MY OWN FOLK-ART TRIBUTE TO THE KING. I TRIED TO COVER THE SPECTRUM OF ELVIS MUSIC— COUNTRY, ROCK, R&B, AND A LOT OF VEGAS. THE ICING IS PAINTED WITH POWDERED FOOD COLOR TO LOOK LIKE BLUE SUEDE. TURQUOISE STONES (JELLYBEANS) AND STUDS (DRAGÉES) FRAME ELVIS'S FACE, WITH A GOLD-LAMÉ BORDER—A NOD TO THOSE FABULOUS JUMPSUITS. THIS PARTICULAR ELVIS IS DEDICATED TO MY MOM—SHE AND ELVIS GO WAY BACK!

TIMING TIPS
● ● ●

These portraits are very time-consuming. They involve quite a few detailed steps, and on top of that, since royal icing decorations are so fragile, I always make at least one backup portrait plaque in case the first one breaks. There's a way to cheat, though: leave the wax paper backing on the portrait, then when the cake's ready to be eaten, lift the picture and peel it off.

CAKE

- 8-inch (20 cm) square, 3 inches (8 cm) high

DECORATIONS

- Dragées: 3 mm and 5 mm
- Royal icing (page 127)
- Fondant (page 128)
- Gum paste banner (page 129)
- Cornstarch (for coating fondant work surfaces)
- Powdered food color: royal blue, black, red, pink, brown, and white petal dust; gold and peacock blue luster dust
- Lemon extract
- Colored sanding sugar: yellow and red
- Jellybeans: turquoise and lime green

EQUIPMENT

- Cake boards: 8-inch (20 cm) square
- Base: 10-inch (25 cm) square
- Decoration template for face (page 132)
- Icing tips: #2, #3, #5, and #6 round; #27 star
- Icing bags and couplers
- Craft paintbrushes
- Toothpicks
- Turntable
- Rolling pin
- Metal spatula
- Electric mixer
- Bench scraper
- Icing smoother
- Wax paper
- Drafting tape (any removable tape)

TECHNIQUES YOU'LL USE
● ● ●

Slicing, filling, and coating a cake (page 22)

● ● ●

Covering with fondant (page 24)

● ● ●

Piping techniques; borders (page 29), flooding (page 33)

● ● ●

Gum-paste decorations (page 33)

● ● ●

Painting with food color (page 34)

● ● ●

Using templates (page 35)

IN ADVANCE

■ ■ ■

1 Make the royal icing Elvis plaque (see A, B, and C, opposite). Let dry overnight.
2 Pipe out a line of stars with a #4 round tip, and flood with thinned royal icing
(page 127). **3** Paint the face with powdered food color mixed with lemon extract.
Color irises of the eyes with the peacock blue luster dust using a fine-tip brush.
Mix the flesh tone color by combining small amounts of pink, brown, and white
food color. For the shadows, add a touch more brown to the mix. Paint the face
with the flesh color and the lips and shadows with the browner flesh color.
4 Paint the shirt with red powdered food color mixed with lemon extract, and
the jacket with a few coats of gold luster dust. Paint star gold. **5 Make the gum-
paste banner** (see D, opposite). Let dry overnight. **6** Paint the banner with a
mixture of gold luster dust and lemon extract. **7** Pipe Viva! across the banner
when the food color is dry, and paint with black food coloring.

8. Bake and cool cake completely.

9. Attach the cake to its boards. Chill, fill,
and apply crumb coat.

10. Cover the cake with fondant. Let set.

11. Place on cake base and secure
with icing.

12. Sponge paint the cake. Mix the royal
blue powdered food color with lemon
extract to make a syrupy paint and
sponge-paint the surface of the fondant.
Once it's dry, you can give it another coat
to make the color dense.

13. Attach the Elvis portrait to the top center
of the cake with a few dots of royal icing.

**14. Make the dragée and jellybean bor-
ders around the portrait.** Start by piping
a line of beaded icing, a little at a time,
along top and side edges of the plaque
using the #3 tip. Add the 3 mm dragées
as you go around forming a continuous
border. Make the next row by attaching
a line of 5 mm dragées, placing one at
every third dragée in the previous row.
Attach a row of jellybeans spaced between
every other 5 mm dragée. Make two more
rows of dragées, using the main cake
photo as a guide.

15. Pipe the gold borders. using the #27
star decorating tip, pipe a reversed shell
border around the top edge of the cake.
Using the #6 round decorating tip, pipe
a heart border around the bottom and up
the sides of the cake. Let dry completely.

16. Paint the borders with a mixture of
gold luster dust and lemon extract.

17. Add the star and the little half-jelly-
bean and dragée pattern to the corners.

A | PIPING THE OUTLINES

Tape the template onto a flat board. Tape all four corners of a piece of wax paper to the template with drafting tape. Trace the lines of the portrait using the #2 decorating tip. Let dry completely.

B | PAINT ICING OUTLINE

Mix black food color with lemon extract, and using a fine-line paintbrush make the outlines black.

C | FILL IN PORTRAIT

Pipe a line of icing using the #5 round tip to make the frame of the portrait. While still wet, cover with yellow sanding sugar and let set. Gently shake off excess sugar. Repeat with red sugar background by first flooding background with thinned royal icing and then sprinkling with red sugar; let set. Using the #3 round tip and working from the upper left-hand corner outward, pipe dots of white royal icing to fill in face, hair, and clothing.

D | CREATE GUM-PASTE BANNER

Using a rolling pin, roll a sheet of gum paste about $\frac{1}{16}$ inch (1.5 mm) thick and $5\frac{1}{2}$ inches (14 cm) long. Cut a strip $\frac{3}{4}$ inch (2 cm) wide; then cut a triangle from both ends. Dry on two little pieces of crumpled paper towel to create curves.

BABY FACE CAKE

I BASED THIS DESIGN ON A WONDERFUL, TIGHTLY CROPPED PHOTOGRAPH OF MY NEPHEW COLE. WE HAVE IT FRAMED IN THE BEDROOM, AND THE FIRST THING I SEE WHEN I WAKE UP IN THE MORNING IS COLE'S HEART-WARMING FACE WITH HIS BIG SWEET EYES AND HIS CUTE CROOKED LITTLE SMILE. I MADE THIS CAKE PORTRAIT BY SMOOTHING OUT BUTTERCREAM WITH A PAINTBRUSH. SINCE LITTLE KIDS' FACES ARE SO SMOOTH THEM-SELVES, THEY'RE PERFECT FOR THIS TECHNIQUE. THE MORE YOU CAN SIM-PLIFY THE SHAPES AND THE FEWER OUTLINES YOU INCLUDE, THE BETTER.

TIMING TIPS

• • •

There isn't any advance decoration work on this cake, unless you decide to make your own template. Allow for some extra chilling time; this cake needs to be thoroughly chilled three separate times for trimming, filling, and icing. Give yourself at least a full day to transfer the outlines from the template to the cake and fill them in with buttercream.

CAKE

- 8-inch (20 cm) square, 2 inches (5 cm) high

DECORATIONS

- Buttercream icing (page 126)
- Paste food color: black, blue, yellow, pink, and apricot
- Cocoa powder (to color icing)

EQUIPMENT

- Cake boards: 8-inch (20 cm) square trimmed to 6 × 8 inches (15 × 20 cm)
- Decoration template for face (page 133)
- Icing tips: #2, #3, and #5 round
- Icing bags and couplers
- Craft paintbrushes
- Toothpicks
- Turntable
- Metal spatula
- Electric mixer

TECHNIQUES YOU'LL USE

• • •

Slicing, filling, and coating a cake (page 22)

• • •

Piping techniques (page 29)

• • •

Using templates (page 35)

66

This is the photo of Cole that the template for this cake was drawn from.

• • •

7. Pipe the black outlines using the #2 decorating tip. To make the black buttercream for outlines, add 1 tablespoon of cocoa to $\frac{1}{4}$ cup (60 gm) of the buttercream, and then add the black paste food coloring. It will taste better, and you'll use a lot less food color.

8. Fill in the blue of the eyes with the #2 round tip. Smooth out the icing with a detail brush moistened with water. Repeat with the eyebrows and lips in yellow and pink with the #2 round tip, and smooth icing.

9. Create the flesh-tone color by mixing small amounts of apricot, pink, and just a touch of yellow food color into the buttercream.

10. Fill in the face, ear, and neck by piping lines of flesh-tone icing back and forth on a diagonal, using the #2 round tip. It's important to work in very small areas (about 1 square inch at a time) because as the icing dries it becomes impossible to smooth out. While the icing is still wet, use a medium round paintbrush moistened with water to smooth over the piped icing. Be careful not to smudge the black by touching it with the wet brush.

11. Fill in the baby blue shirt by piping lines of icing using the #3 round decorating tip. Do not smooth out the texture of the shirt.

12. Pipe the borders. Start by piping a yellow line around the black edge of the design. Use a #5 tip. Then pipe rows of beaded borders around that using the #3 tip. Pipe one row at the top and bottom of the face, and three rows on either side.

13. Using the #5 round decorating tip, pipe alternating colored (blue, pink, and yellow) beads as the bottom border of the cake.

1. Bake and cool cake completely.

2. Set, but do not attach, the square cake onto a cake board for easier handling, and chill thoroughly.

3. Trim the square to size. Cut a 2-inch (5 cm) strip off the side of the cake so that the cake measures 6 × 8 inches (15 × 20 cm).

4. Attach the cake to its board, fill, and apply crumb coat; chill again.

5. Ice the cake. Once the crumb coating is set, cover the cake in an even layer of white buttercream and chill again for at least 2 hours.

6. Gently place the template on top of the cake. Pin all four corners to hold it in place. Transfer the template design onto the cake by making pinholes following the lines of the template. Carefully remove the paper, and you have a guideline for piping your design.

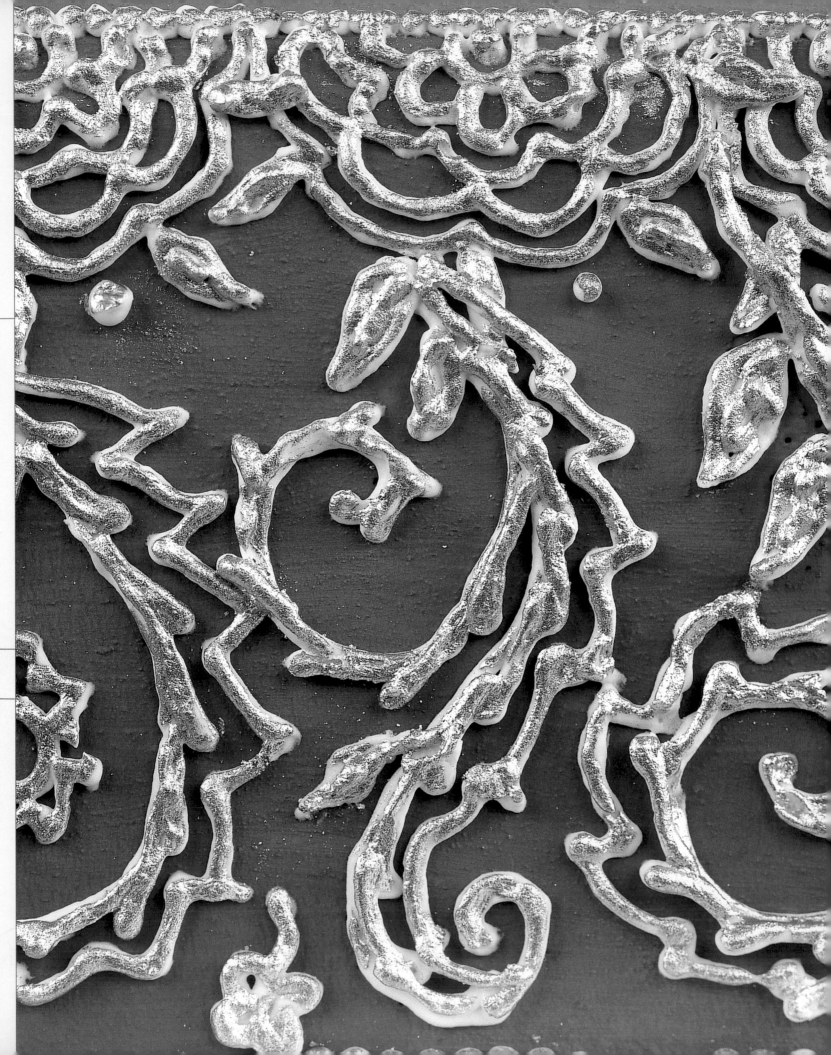

Tiers of Happiness

If there's anything better than getting a cake,

it's getting a cake made from a whole bunch of cakes, stacked up on top of each other. It's an over-the-top sensation loaded with symbolism, love...and buttah!

Tiered cakes are great for special occasions: important birthdays, anniversaries, bar mitzvahs, christenings, and, of course, weddings. I love making these cakes for important moments in the lives of my family and friends: the cake itself becomes an integral part of the festivity. The size and scale of a tiered cake can make it the focal point of a celebration in a big space like a restaurant, a catering hall, or a hotel ball-room. A tiered cake stands out, even when you see it across the room.

When planning a cake for a special event, try to incorporate details from the loca-tion into the cake. Color or decorating themes from the room, flowers from the cen-terpieces, or fabric from a dress can all inspire elements of the cake's design. I've always found fabrics and textiles a great inspiration—once, when designing a cake for a '70s-theme party, I decided to work in the very '70s texture of the shag carpet-ing. Of course, you aren't limited to any single design element: the great thing about a multitiered cake is that it gives you a big canvas to mix textures and colors.

When it comes to making a wedding cake, you've got a lot of tradition and sym-bolism working for you. It goes all the way back to weddings in ancient Rome, where wheat was a symbol of fertility and prosperity, and the guests would actually throw cake at the bride. It puts a nicer light on the current custom of the groom squishing a piece of cake into the bride's face.

Closer to modern times, there's a Victorian wedding-cake custom, called a ribbon pull, that I've used in cakes for many occasions. You hide small silver charms, attached to ribbons, under the cake's bottom tier. In the nineteenth century, the bridesmaids would each pull a ribbon and get a token of their fortune: a wedding ring for the next to marry, horseshoes and clovers for good luck, anchors for hope or adventure, thimbles for old maid. I've changed this tradition slightly: I never include a thimble—it just seems mean!—but I double up on hearts and good-luck charms. The idea also works wonderfully for a young girl's birthday cake, with a slightly dif-ferent assortment of charms—horses, flowers, ballerinas, and all the lucky charms. Little girls love it!

FLOWER CAKE

THIS IS A LESS IS MORE DESIGN—A MODERN CAKE WITH CLEAN AND MINI-MALIST LINES. EACH TIER HAS A DIFFERENT ICONIC SHAPE, WITH LITTLE ADDITIONAL ADORNMENT—NO PIPED BORDERS, NO EDIBLE SCULPTURES. WHEN THE CAKE IS VIEWED FROM ABOVE, IT LOOKS LIKE A FLOWER WITH A CREAM-COLORED CENTER AND FUCHSIA PETALS. IF YOU USE A CAKE TOPPER, IT'S IMPORTANT THAT IT BE SLEEK AND ELEGANT AS WELL, LIKE THIS CLASSIC BRIDE AND GROOM.

TIMING TIPS

The gum-paste cutout flowers can be made anywhere from one day to two weeks ahead of time. Allow the fondant on the petal tier to set overnight before painting it. Since there aren't any piped borders, it's particularly important to take your time and make a straight, clean edge when you cut the bottom of the fondant.

CAKE

- 4-inch (10 cm) heart tier, 2 inches (5 cm) high
- 9-inch (23 cm) round tier, 2 inches (5 cm) high
- 12-inch (30 cm) petal tier, 4 inches (10 cm) high

DECORATIONS

- Gum-paste decorations: 8 flower cutouts
- Fondant (page 128)
- Cornstarch (for coating work surfaces)
- Paste food color: ivory
- Powdered food color: orange and red petal dust, fuchsia luster dust
- Lemon extract
- Bride-and-groom cake topper (optional)

EQUIPMENT

- Cake boards: 5-, 9-, and 12-inch (13, 23, and 30 cm) round boards
- Cake stand or 14-inch (35 cm) base
- Icing tips: #3 and #4 round
- Icing bags and couplers
- Cookie cutter: flower
- 90-degree triangle
- Tracing wheel
- Craft paintbrushes
- Scissors
- Plastic straws
- Rolling pin
- Metal spatula
- Electric mixer
- Bench scraper
- Icing smoother

TECHNIQUES YOU'LL USE

Slicing, filling, and coating a cake (page 22)

Covering with fondant (page 24)

Building a tiered cake (page 26)

Gum-paste decorations (page 33)

Painting with food color (page 34)

IN ADVANCE
· · ·

1 **Make the gum-paste flowers.** Color the gum paste by kneading in a small amount of ivory paste food color. Roll out the gum paste to $\frac{1}{16}$-inch (1.5 mm) thickness and cut out eight flowers with the cookie cutter. Let dry. These flowers are not molded to look like real flowers, but left completely flat (see A, right). **2** Trim the 5- and 14-inch (13 and 35 cm) round cake boards to the shapes of their tiers. Place the 4-inch (10 cm) heart and the 12-inch (30 cm) petal cake pans on top of their boards and trace the bottom outline of the pan onto the boards. Cut to shapes.

3. Bake and cool cakes completely.

4. Attach the cakes to their boards. Chill, fill, and apply crumb coat.

5. Color the fondant for all three tiers by adding a small amount of ivory paste food color a little at a time, kneading the fondant until the color is even.

6. **Cover the tiers in fondant.** Start with the largest tier. Seal fondant in plastic between each tier and set aside until ready to cover next tier. Let the round and petal-shaped tiers set.

7. Make a quilted pattern on the heart-shaped tier (see B, right).

8. Attach the petal tier to the base or cake stand.

9. **Paint the petal-shaped tier.** Coat the sides of the cake in smooth, even strokes. Blend orange powdered food color with a touch of red and combine with lemon extract. Once it's dry, you can give it another coat to make the color opaque. Paint the top surface of the petal tier with fuchsia luster dust mixed with lemon extract. Let dry.

10. Cut support straws to size and insert them into the 9- and 12-inch (23 and 30 cm) tiers.

11. Center, stack, and attach the tiers to each other, and the bride and groom to the top of the cake, with icing.

12. **Attach the gum-paste flowers** to the side of cake by brushing very small dots of water on the backs of the flower centers and then gently pressing for a few seconds to adhere to fondant. Let set.

A | DETAIL OF FLOWERS

B | CREATE A QUILTED PATTERN

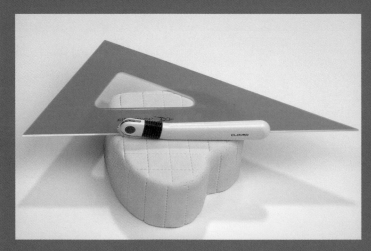

Place a triangle diagonally on top of the cake. Run the tracing wheel along the edge of the triangle to emboss dotted lines (about 1 inch [2.5 cm] apart) across the fondant. Use these lines as guides to emboss lines crossing in the other direction. To make the vertical lines along the side of the cake, align the bottom edge of the triangle with the bottom edge of the cake and emboss lines along the vertical edge of the triangle.

72

WHITE CHRISTMAS

THIS CAKE STARTED WITH THE VINTAGE CAKE TOPPER AND THE IDEA TO CREATE A RATTANLIKE BASKET-WEAVE PATTERN. I WAS PLANNING TO PAINT IT DIFFERENT SHADES OF TAN AND BEIGE, BUT SINCE IT WAS THE BEGINNING OF DECEMBER, WHITE JUST SEEMED RIGHT. FOR THE CAKE'S CORSAGE, RATHER THAN IMITATING REAL FLOWERS, I TRIED FOR A LOOK OF CARVED AND PAINTED WOOD TO COMPLEMENT THE RATTAN.

CAKE

- 6-inch (15 cm) round tier, 3 inches (8 cm) high
- 8-inch (20 cm) round tier, 3 inches (8 cm) high
- 10-inch (25 cm) round tier, 3 inches (7 cm) high

DECORATIONS

- Gum-paste decorations: 2 flowers
- Royal icing (page 127)
- Cornstarch (for coating work surfaces)
- Fondant (page 128)
- Celeri sugar beads or piped balls of royal icing*
- Bride-and-groom cake topper (optional)

EQUIPMENT

- Cake boards: 6-, 8-, and 10-inch (15, 20, and 25 cm) round boards
- Cake stand (optional) or 12-inch (30 cm) base
- Icing tips: #4, #7, #8 (optional), and #9 round
- Icing bags and couplers
- Gum-paste cutters: $1\frac{1}{2}$-, $1\frac{7}{8}$-, and $2\frac{1}{4}$-inch (4, 5, and 6 cm) fluted circles; small bud
- Wax paper
- Plastic straws
- Rolling pin
- Metal spatula
- Electric mixer
- Bench scraper
- Icing smoother

TECHNIQUES YOU'LL USE

■ ■ ■

Slicing, filling, and coating a cake
(page 22)

■ ■ ■

Covering with fondant
(page 24)

■ ■ ■

Building a tiered cake
(page 26)

■ ■ ■

Piping techniques
(page 29)

■ ■ ■

Gum-paste decorations
(page 33)

TIMING TIPS

■ ■ ■

The flowers are simple cookie-cutter shapes, and the swirls are very basic. Once you've got the repeated basket-weave pattern down, this is a fairly easy cake to finish, but it's still a good idea to set aside a day for decorating.

IN ADVANCE

■ ■ ■

1 **Make the gum-paste flowers** (see A, opposite). **2** Make the royal icing swirls with tiny flower buds (see B, opposite).

---

3. Bake and cool cakes completely.

4. Attach the cakes to their boards. Chill, fill, and apply crumb coat.

5. Cover the tiers in fondant. Let the fondant set.

6. Attach the bottom tier to the base or cake stand.

7. Cut support straws to size and insert them into the 8- (20 cm) and 10-inch (25 cm) tiers.

8. Pipe rattan patterns. Using a #7 tip for the top tier, and #9 round decorating tip for the bottom tier, pipe the patterns on the sides of the tiers (see C, opposite). Let set.

9. Center, stack, and attach the tiers to each other with icing.

10. Attach the gum-paste flowers and the royal icing swirls on the front and to the side of the 6-inch (15 cm) tier with dots of royal icing (see D, opposite). Let set.

11. Attach the celeri beads in three concentric rows on top of the bottom tier with dots of royal icing.

12. Position porcelain young lovers on top of cake.

The tiny celeri sugar beads used to decorate this cake have a great texture, but if you prefer, you can get a similar effect by piping balls of royal icing with a #8 round decorating tip in place of the beads.

A | MAKE THE GUM-PASTE FLOWERS

Roll out the gum paste to $\frac{1}{16}$-inch (1.5 mm) thickness and cut the scalloped circle shapes with fluted circle cutters. Let dry completely flat. Attach the three circles on top of each other from smallest to largest with a few drops of water. Attach four celeri beads to the centers of each flower with dots of royal icing.

B | MAKE SWIRLS AND TINY BUDS

Pipe swirls of royal icing using the #4 round tip. Each swirl consists of two lines of icing piped on top of each other (for added strength).

Cut out gum-paste buds and shape petals with ball tool. Brush small dot of water in the centers of buds to adhere bead centers, and dry buds on top of celeri beads. Attach to completely hardened swirls with dots of royal icing.

C | PIPE RATTAN PATTERN

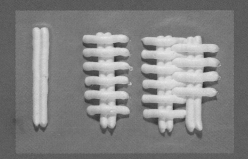

Using round decorating tips, pipe a straight vertical line. Next, pipe a series of short horizontal lines, each about 1 inch (2.5 cm) long, centered across the vertical line. Pipe another vertical, then another row of horizontal lines, filling in the spaces left open in the previous set of horizontal lines. (Continue until you've covered the surface.)

D | DETAIL OF FLOWER DECORATIONS ON TOP TIER

SAMMY & LULU

WHEN I WAS CHECKING OUT ARRANGEMENTS FOR MY WEDDING, A FLORIST SHOWED ME A WOODEN BOX WITH PLANTED WHEAT GRASS AS A BASE FOR AN UNUSUAL FLORAL TREATMENT. I DIDN'T USE IT FOR MY OWN CERE-MONY, BUT IT DID INSPIRE THIS WHIMSICAL WEDDING CAKE. GREEN GRASS, A SKY OF BLUE WITH WHITE PUFFY CLOUDS, AND FANTASIES OF HAPPILY EVER AFTER ACCOMPANY SAMMY AND LULU ON THEIR WEDDING DAY.

TIMING TIPS
...

Believe it or not, there are about 600 individually piped blades of icing grass on top of the cake. Since you need to rest your hands periodically from the repeated motion, it takes about three sittings to complete them. The grass, gum-paste flowers, and leaves should be made three days to two weeks in advance. It also takes some time to "plant" the grass on the top of the cake.

CAKE

- 6-inch (15 cm) square tier, 3 inches (8 cm) high
- 9-inch (23 cm) hexagonal tier, 3 inches (8 cm) high
- 12-inch (30 cm) hexagonal tier, 3 inches (8 cm) high

DECORATIONS

- Gum-paste decorations: 6 large daisies, 60 small blossoms, 28 rose leaves, 2 large leaves (lily cutter), 1 fluted oval plaque (for lettering)
- Powdered food color: gold luster dust; gold iridescent powder; brown, and yellow petal dust
- Paste food color: green, pink
- Lemon extract
- Royal icing (page 127)
- Cornstarch (for coating work surfaces)
- Fondant (page 128)
- Bride-and-groom cake topper (optional)

EQUIPMENT

- Cake boards: 6-inch (15 cm) square, 9-inch (23 cm) and 12-inch (30 cm) round boards
- Base: 14-inch (35 cm) foam-core base
- Small craft jewelry box: $1\frac{1}{2}$-inches × $2\frac{1}{2}$-inches (4 cm × 6 cm) and 1 inch (2.5 cm) high (standard earring-box size)
- Icing tips: #2, #3, and #6 round
- Icing bags and couplers
- Gum-paste cutters: plunger daisy, small blossom, rose leaf, lily, 5-inch (13 cm) fluted oval, and 3-inch (8 cm) circle
- Ball tool
- Veining mat
- Wax paper
- Skewers
- Plastic straws
- Wax paper
- Rolling pin
- Metal spatula
- Electric mixer
- Bench scraper
- Icing smoother

TECHNIQUES YOU'LL USE
— ... —

Slicing, filling, and coating a cake (page 22)

...

Covering with fondant (page 24)

...

Building a tiered cake (page 26)

...

Piping techniques (page 29)

...

Gum-paste decorations (page 33)

...

Painting with food color (page 34)

IN ADVANCE

1 Make the large gum-paste flowers (see A, opposite). **2** Cut out the large and small leaves and the blossoms. Press a veining pad into the small leaves to create veined texture. Gently press the ball tool into the flowers to give them a curved shape. Using the #3 round decorating tip, pipe a dot of icing into the center of each small flower and let dry. **3** Pipe approximately 600 blades of grass (see B, opposite). **4** Make a small camouflaged platform for the bride and groom to stand on. Take the craft (cardboard) jewelry box and pipe rows of green dots to cover the top. (The platform will be centered on top of the cake and the blades of grass will be attached around it.) **5** Decorate the oval plaque by piping the names in pink royal icing with the #2 round decorating tip and a pink line border around the edge with the #3 round tip. Paint the lettering, but not the "&," brown. **6 Complete the Sammy & Lulu flower.** Center a skewer about $\frac{1}{4}$ inch (6 mm) from the top in the back of the plaque to form a stem. Fasten the plaque to a skewer with a generous piping of royal icing. Attach the large leaves under and on either side of the plaque with a few dots of royal icing. Let dry facedown on a piece of wax paper. **7** Trim the 9- and 12-inch (23 and 30 cm) round cake boards to the shapes of their tiers. Place the hexagon cake pans on top of their boards and copy the bottom outline of the pan onto the boards with a pencil. Cut the shapes.

8. Bake and cool cakes completely.

9. Attach the cakes to their boards. Chill, fill, and apply crumb coat.

10. Cover the tiers in fondant starting with the smallest tier.

11. For the 9-inch (23 cm) tier, mix pink paste food color with the fondant, and cover the tier.

12. Create guidelines for piping royal icing. For the largest tier: while the fondant is still soft, gently trace swags. Use the 3-inch (8 cm) circle cutter to make light scores for the swags. Let the fondant set.

13. Set on base. Center and attach the bottom tier to the foam-core base with royal icing.

14. Paint the tiers. For the square tier, mix gold luster dust with lemon extract to create a thin, syruplike consistency. Use a medium or small-sized flat craft brush and paint with smooth, even strokes. Once it's dry, give it another coat to build up the density.

15. For the largest tier, paint the half circle inside the swags with a mixture of gold iridescent powder and lemon extract. Paint the background with brown powdered food color mixed with lemon extract. Once it's dry, give it another coat.

16. Attach the blades of grass to the top of the cake. First, attach the iced jewelry box centered on the top tier to form a solid platform for the bride-and-groom cake topper.

17. Pipe a line of green royal icing along the top left edge of the square tier. While the icing is wet, insert one blade at a time into the icing so that it stands up like grass (see C, opposite). Continue piping one row of icing at a time parallel to the first row and attaching blades of grass until the top of the cake is covered (work around the box so that it is also surrounded by grass). Let set.

18. Attach border of small leaves along top edge of cake with royal icing so that the front tip of each leaf is slightly overlapped by the next leaf.

19. Affix a blossom on the center of each leaf with a dot of royal icing.

20. Cut support straws to size and insert them into the hexagonal tiers.

21. Stack the tiers. Center, stack, and attach the tiers to each other with icing.

22. Attach one large gum-paste flower to the center of each of the sides of the pink hexagonal tier with dots of royal icing. Let set.

23. Pipe the royal icing borders. For the square and the 9-inch (23 cm) tiers: Using the #3 round decorating tip, pipe beaded borders down the corner edges of the square and hexagon. Pipe snail trail borders using the #6 round decorating tip around the bottom of both tiers and the top of the 9-inch (23 cm) tier.

24. For the bottom tier, use the #2 round decorating tip to pipe a tiny snail trail border outlining the swags. Use the #6 round decorating tip to pipe a snail trail border along the bottom edge of the cake.

25. Attach the blossoms. Place at each corner of the square, hexagons, and at each intersection of the swags with a dot of royal icing. Let set.

26. Paint the centers of the blossoms with yellow powdered food color mixed with lemon extract.

27. Attach the bride-and-groom cake topper (optional) with a few dots of royal icing.

A | MAKE THE DAISY AND PLAQUE

Roll out the gum paste to $\frac{1}{16}$-inch (1.5 mm) thickness, and cut out daisies and the fluted oval shapes with gum-paste cutters. Let dry flat.

B | PIPE BLADES OF GRASS

Use the #6 decorating tip to pipe 1-inch (2.5 cm) lines of royal icing onto wax paper and let dry for twenty-four hours. Carefully peel off the wax paper backing from the blades of grass.

C | DETAIL OF TOP TIER

79

JACKPOT!

THIS CAKE HAS A VERY SPECIAL PLACE IN MY HEART. JUST BEFORE MY HUSBAND AND I STARTED DATING, I MENTIONED THAT I WAS WORKING ON A WEDDING CAKE, AND HE ASKED IF I HAD A BRIDE-AND-GROOM TOPPER FOR IT YET. I DIDN'T, SO THE NEXT DAY HE SURPRISED ME AND SENT THIS ONE OVER TO MY OFFICE. HE'D USED IT FOR A PHOTO SHOOT AND IT WAS THE BEST SET OF BRIDE AND GROOM FIGURES I'D EVER SEEN. MY ASSISTANT, JAMIE, TOOK ONE LOOK AT IT AND SAID VERY MATTER-OF-FACTLY, "NOW, THAT'S A SIGN IF EVER I'VE SEEN ONE." (I WAS SKEPTICAL.) THREE YEARS LATER WE WERE MARRIED, AND THIS IS ONE OF THE CAKES WE HAD AT OUR WEDDING—JACKPOT!

TIMING TIPS

...

Most of the decoration for this cake are made before the cake is ever baked. All the royal icing and gum-paste decorations can be made weeks in advance, and should be made at least three days in advance. Give yourself a full day after the fondant is on the cake to attach the decorations, because you want to make sure the royal icing "glue" has time to set (especially the little skirt of almonds) before moving it.

CAKE

- 5-inch (13 cm) round tier, 3 inches (8 cm) high
- 7-inch (18 cm) round tier, 3 inches (8 cm) high
- 9-inch (23 cm) round tier, 2 inches (5 cm) high
- 12-inch (30 cm) round tier, 4 inches (10 cm) high

DECORATIONS

- Dragées: small (3 mm), medium (4 mm), and large (5 mm) silver balls; silver oval dragées
- 1 pound (0.5 kg) silver-coated Jordan almonds (or substitute large chocolate silver dragées that are about the same shape)
- Gum-paste decorations: ten $2\frac{1}{4}$-inch (6 cm) hearts; thirty-six $1\frac{1}{2}$-inch (4 cm) circles; one butterfly

- Powdered food color: pearl white luster dust, silver highlighter, gold sparkle (optional), red and black petal dust
- Lemon extract
- Royal icing (see page 127)
- 5-inch (13 cm) plastic heart
- Bride-and-groom cake topper
- Two skewers
- Ribbon: $1\frac{1}{2}$ yards (1.4 m) of $1\frac{1}{2}$-inch (4 cm) red satin ribbon; $1\frac{1}{2}$ yards (1.4 m) of $\frac{3}{4}$-inch (2 cm) red satin ribbon
- Fondant (page 128)
- Cornstarch for coating work surface

EQUIPMENT

- Cake boards: 5-, 7-, 9-, and 12-inch (13, 18, 23, and 30 cm) separator boards
- Base: 14-inch (35 cm) silver foil-covered foam-core base

- Decoration template for lettering (page 132)
- Plastic straws
- Icing tips: #3, #5 round
- Icing bag and coupler
- Craft paintbrushes
- Gum-paste cutters: $1\frac{1}{2}$-inch (4 cm) circle, $2\frac{1}{4}$-inch (6 cm) heart shape, butterfly (or use template)
- Rolling pin
- Metal spatula
- Wax paper
- Ruler
- Scissors
- Hot glue gun
- 10-inch (25 cm) square piece of cardboard
- Turntable
- Standing electric mixer
- Bench scraper
- Icing smoother

TECHNIQUES YOU'LL USE

IN ADVANCE
■ ■ ■

1 **Make the royal icing decorations.** Let dry overnight (the lettering will require two separate twelve-hour drying periods; once when you make the royal icing decorations, and again after you attach to the skewers). Cut two skewers $6\frac{1}{4}$ inches (15.5 cm) long and paint them with a mixture of black food coloring and lemon extract. Pipe the lettering (see A, opposite). When the letters are completely dry, attach them to the skewers with royal icing and let dry again (see B, opposite). **2** Attach the back of the skewers to the plastic heart with a hot glue gun. Affix 4 mm and 5 mm dragées to outlines of plastic heart with royal icing. **3** Make 40 dragée starbursts (see C, opposite). **4** Cut out the gum-paste hearts, circles, and butterfly. Let dry. **5** **Paint the gum-paste decorations.** Mix 4 parts pearl white luster dust with 1 part silver highlighter and lemon extract, and paint the hearts and circles. (Optional: when silver and pearl dries on hearts, dust with gold sparkle on dry paintbrush for "hearts of gold.") Paint the butterfly with a mixture of red petal dust and lemon extract. **6** Attach a $\frac{3}{4}$-inch (2 cm) ribbon to the edge of the foamcore base and a $1\frac{1}{2}$-inch (4 cm) bow to back of base with hot glue gun. **7** Create a support board for the almond border for when the icing is setting. Place a 7-inch (18 cm) cake pan on top of the 10-inch (25 cm) square piece of cardboard, and trace the outline of the pan. Cut out the center circle and discard. Cut remaining cardboard piece in half and put aside.

8. Bake and cool cakes completely.

9. Attach the cakes to cake boards. Chill, fill, and apply crumb coat.

10. Cover the cakes with fondant. Let the fondant set.

11. Center and attach the 12-inch (30 cm) tier to the foam-core base with royal icing.

12. Cut support straws to size and insert them into the 7-, 9-, and 12-inch (18, 23, and 30 cm) tiers.

13. Center and stack the 5-inch (13 cm) tier on top of the 7-inch (18 cm) tier.

14. Attach a row of the silver dragée starbursts that are evenly spaced approximately $\frac{1}{2}$ inch (13 mm) apart around the top outside edge of the cake. Add a second row of starbursts along the adjacent top edge of the cake, using the photograph (page 84) as a guide.

15. **Make the silver almond border.** Using royal icing, attach the silver-coated almonds to the top edge of the 7-inch (18 cm) cake to make the bottom border for the 5-inch (13 cm) tier (the two tiers must be stacked already). Attach one 4 mm dragée between each of the almonds. The almonds are a little heavy and need extra support while setting. Set prepared cardboard support in place, like a miniature scaffolding, next to the cake. Use cups or glasses to hold up the cardboard supports at the desired height. After the almonds have set (overnight), remove the supports.

16. Pipe a line of royal icing dots with the #3 tip and attach two rows of 3 mm dragées at the bottom of the 7-inch (18 cm) tier. Starting with bottom row, pipe five dots, add dragées, and then pipe

five more, and so on until borders are complete. Attach a third row above that, spacing one dragée over every other dragée in the row below it.

17. Add a small symmetrical pattern of dragées above the previous rows, as if they were little fizzles of champagne bubbles, with one dragée positioned over the center of each pair below (see page 84 for reference).

18. **Attach gum-paste circles** in two rows to the 12-inch (30 cm) tier with royal icing approximately $\frac{1}{2}$ inch (13 mm) from the top, the bottom, and in between each set of touching circles. This can be done by eye, or you can measure pattern in advance with a ruler and mark the fondant lightly with a toothpick.

19. Attach hearts to the 9-inch (23 cm) tier, also spacing them about $\frac{1}{2}$ inch (13 mm) apart.

20. Stack the remaining tiers.

21. Add icing and dragée trims to bottoms of the 9- and 12-inch (23 and 30 cm) tiers. Pipe a line of beaded icing along the bottom of the 9-inch (23 cm) tier using the #5 tip. Add 3 mm dragées above and between every other icing bead. Attach a row of 5 mm dragées along the bottom of the 12-inch (30 cm) tier, then a second row above that, skipping every other space, and finish by attaching a few sets of 3 mm dragées just above this row and between the circles of gum paste.

22. **Set up the happy couple!** Attach the plastic heart, bride and groom, and butterfly to the top of the cake with royal icing. Secure heart by placing toothpicks in front and behind as needed. To camouflage them, pipe royal icing dots over exposed portion of toothpicks and add 5mm dragees. The butterfly will hide them, too.

A | PIPE THE LETTERING

Tape a sheet of wax paper over the lettering template. Using a #3 tip, trace the lettering in royal icing and let dry for two to three hours.

B | COMPLETE THE MARQUEE

One letter at a time, gently attach #3 dragées with a second layer of icing. Icing hardens quickly, so work in small sections. When dry (overnight), gently lift each letter from the wax paper. Pipe icing along the back of the letters and attach to the skewers.

C | MAKE STARBURSTS

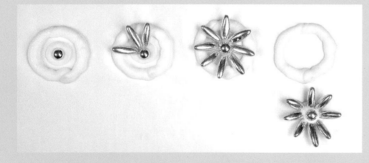

- Using a #5 round tip, pipe forty-five 1-inch (2.5 cm) rings onto wax paper (as temporary supports for starburst shapes). When dry (overnight), pipe a large dot of icing in center of circle; place 5 mm dragée in middle.

- While dot is still wet, place oval dragées into icing around center dragée, with the outer ends propped upwards on the dry support rings.

- Continue adding a total of eight oval dragées around center. Let dry overnight.

- Gently lift the starbursts from the wax paper, leaving the supports behind.

VARIATION

A little Vegas, a little Fred and Ginger; this smaller version of the Jackpot! cake shows how the silver dragées and silver-coated Jordan almonds create tiny bursts and bubbles of sparkling light at an evening wedding, catching the lights of candles or other dramatic lighting you may have in the room. The Jackpot marquee can seem as if it's made up of tiny electric lights. Aside from the size, the other variation in this cake is that I covered the butterfly in tiny dragées to add even more shimmer. You can do this by piping an outline of royal icing on the red butterfly wings (before they are added to the icing body) and then flooding with flow-consistency icing. While the icing is still wet, sprinkle liberally with dragées and pat them down into the icing. Let dry completely and attach to the body, which can also be covered in dragées.

DOGWOODS & BUTTERFLIES

I LOVE THE ANIMATED QUALITY OF BOTH BUTTERFLIES AND DOGWOODS. HERE, BRIGHT RED GUM-PASTE BUTTERFLIES AND DOGWOOD FLOWERS DANCE TOGETHER IN AN IMAGINARY BREEZE. SOME REALLY BEAUTIFUL AGENT PROVOCATEUR LINGERIE INSPIRED THE PINK RIBBON AND BOWS AND BLACK-AND-WHITE TRIM.

TIMING TIPS

The gum-paste flowers, butterflies, and bows should be made no less than three days in advance, so you can be sure they're all dry enough to hold their shape. The consistency of the gum paste is particularly important for the dogwood flowers, because if it's too soft, the petals will lie flat on the cake rather than lifting up. The little black-and-white icing flowers should also be made in advance: they're very fragile, so be sure to make extra. The gum-paste ribbons, though, are made just before they go on the cake.

CAKE

- 6-inch (15-cm) round tier, 3 inches (8 cm) high
- 7-inch (18-cm) round tier, 3 inches (8 cm) high

DECORATIONS

- Gum-paste decorations: 24 dogwood flowers, 2 bows, 2 butterflies, and 2 ribbons
- 28 royal icing outline flowers
- Small dragées (3 mm)
- Royal icing for piping (page 127)
- Paste food color: pink
- Powdered food color: pink, red, black, and green petal dust; antique white luster dust
- Lemon extract
- Cloth-covered wire cut to four 1-inch (2.5 cm) pieces (for antennae)
- Fondant (page 128)
- Cornstarch for coating work surface

EQUIPMENT

- Cake boards: 6-inch (15 cm) and 7-inch (18 cm) round separator boards
- Cake stand or 8-inch (20 cm) foam-core base
- Icing tips: #3 and #5 round; #13 star
- Icing bags and couplers
- Cutters: dogwood and butterfly
- Craft paintbrushes
- Toothpicks
- Rolling pin
- Metal spatula
- Wax paper
- Electric mixer
- Bench scraper
- Icing smoother

TECHNIQUES YOU'LL USE

Slicing, filling, and coating a cake (page 22)

Covering with fondant (page 24)

Building a tiered cake (page 26)

Piping techniques (page 29)

Gum-paste decorations (page 33)

Painting with food color (page 34)

IN ADVANCE
• • •

1 **Make the gum-paste dogwood flowers and butterflies** (see A and B, page 88).
2 Make the bows. Mix pink paste food color into gum paste for the bows and ribbons. The ribbons are made just before they go on the cake, so set aside just over half of the pink gum paste for the ribbons and seal in plastic. Form bows and let dry with small pieces of paper towel inside the loops to form shape of bow. **3** When the butterflies are dry, paint the wings with two coats of red powdered food color mixed with lemon extract. Paint the body and antennae black.
4 When the dogwoods are dry, add just a touch of pink and black to the edges.
5 **Pipe royal icing outline flowers.** Pipe royal icing outline flowers with five petals each onto wax paper using a #3 round decorating tip. To create the curved shape of the flowers, tape the wax paper over a cylindrical kitchen utensil, like the thick handle of a mixing spoon. When you pipe the flowers they will conform to the shape of the cylinder. Let dry completely and gently peel wax paper from the backs of the flowers. These are very fragile, so make extras.

6. Bake and cool cakes completely.

7. Attach cakes to cake boards. Chill, fill, and apply crumb coat.

8. **Cover the tiers with fondant.** Let fondant set.

9. Center and attach the 7-inch (18 cm) tier to the cake stand (or foam-core base, if you'd prefer not to use a cake stand) with royal icing.

10. Cut support straws to size and insert into the 7-inch (18 cm) tier.

11. Center, stack, and attach the 6-inch (15 cm) tier with icing.

12. Paint the tiers with antique white luster dust mixed with lemon extract.

13. **Attach the ribbons.** Roll out the pink gum paste to about a $\frac{1}{16}$-inch (1.5 mm) thickness and cut a 1-inch × 20-inch (2.5 cm × 50 cm) ribbon to go around the 6-inch (15 cm) tier, and attach with a few drops of water. Cut a 1-inch × 24-inch (2.5 cm × 60 cm) ribbon to go around the 7-inch (18 cm) tier and attach with water. If you find it easier to handle in shorter pieces, the ribbon works just as well if you make it in two or three pieces per tier and make clean-cut seams that meet. You can always cover up a seam with one of the little icing flowers later.

14. **Pipe small shell borders** using the #13 star decorating tip around the tops of both ribbons. Pipe a double border of beads around the bottoms of the ribbons using the #3 tip.

15. Attach the bows to the ribbons with royal icing. Place toothpicks just below the bows to add a little extra support in holding up the bow while the icing is hardening. Once the icing is hard and the bow attached, you can remove the toothpicks and hide the little holes they leave with a dot of royal icing.

16. Pipe borders of dots with the #3 round tip on the edges of the bows.

17. **Paint the borders on the ribbons and bows black.** Paint every other little royal icing flower black as well.

18. Pipe a beaded border around the top of the 6-inch (15 cm) tier and attach a row of dragées just outside the beaded border at every other bead of icing.

19. Attach the dogwoods to the top of the cake in layers overlapping each other. The petals of the flowers closest to the border should also overlap the edge of the cake. You can play around with the arrangement in different patterns before using icing to attach them, to be sure you get an arrangement that you like (see page 88).

20. **Place the butterflies on the flowers.** Remember, the red powdered food color will come off on your hands and the white flowers. The edges of the flowers are painted pink and black, so it's not a big deal if some of the red gets on the edges.

21. Attach the black and white flowers to the ribbons with dots of royal icing, and pipe dots into their centers with the #5 tip.

A | MAKE THE FLOWER CUTOUTS

B | CUT OUT THE BUTTERFLIES

See Basic Instructions on pages 31–32 for shaping petals. Let dry. Pipe dots of green royal icing with the #3 tip to form the stamens: start with a dot in the center. Pipe two rings of dots around it.

Roll out gum-paste and use a butterfly cutter to make the shape. Separate the wings. Let dry. Pipe 1-inch (2.5 cm) line of royal icing with the #5 tip for the body; while still wet, press the wings into sides of the body and antennae into head. Prop into position with small pieces of wadded paper towel until dry.

C | DETAIL OF FLOWERS

PHILADELPHIA STORY

∎ ∎ ∎

While the Dogwoods & Butterflies cake can celebrate any occasion, I wanted to try a variation with a bride-and-groom cake topper. This particular couple fit well with this cake, nestling nicely into its flowers. The topper was mass-produced in the 1930s, which makes it relatively easy to find in online auctions. There are porcelain and metal versions in different sizes. There's a wedding reception in the classic 1940 movie The Philadelphia Story, where each table sports a bouquet of flowers crested with this topper. The only difference is that the groom is holding a top hat.

My topper is a 3-inch-tall (8 cm) metal version. It was almost completely stripped of its original paint, so I repainted it and added some tiny rhinestones to the bride's hair. The topper was very heavy, so I used plastic straws, cut to size, as supports to keep it from sinking into the cake.

When making this cake, you need to make a couple of small changes from the basic Dogwoods & Butterflies procedure. You need to attach the topper to the top center of the cake before adding the flowers. And you'll have to adjust the placement of the butterflies to accommodate the topper.

RED VELVET

I LIKE CAKES THAT APPEAL TO ALL THE SENSES. THIS ONE IS ALL ABOUT TEXTURE—WHEN YOU SEE IT, YOU WANT TO TOUCH IT. BUT I ALSO WANTED IT TO TASTE AS VELVETY AS IT LOOKS. LAYERS OF POWDERED FOOD COLOR ON THE CENTER TIER AND BOW CREATE A PINK, SUEDELIKE SURFACE. TINY RED ICING ROSES FILL THE CLEFTS OF THE LARGE RED FONDANT-COVERED HEARTS. I'VE ALWAYS LOVED PINK AND RED AS A FASHION COMBINATION— IF THIS WERE A DRESS, I'D WEAR IT.

CAKE

- 6-inch (15 cm) heart-shaped tier, 3 inches (8 cm) high
- 8-inch (20 cm) heart-shaped tier, 3 inches (8 cm) high
- 10-inch (25 cm) round tier, 3 inches (8 cm) high
- 12-inch (30 cm) round tier, 4 inches (10 cm) high

DECORATIONS

- 65 to 70 red royal icing roses (always make extra)
- Royal icing (page 127)
- Gum-paste decorations: 1 bow, 20 leaf cutouts
- Paste food color: pink
- Powdered food color: red and pink petal dust, gold iridescent powder, and pink luster dust
- Ribbon: $1\frac{1}{2}$ yards (1.4 m) of $\frac{1}{4}$-inch (6 mm) pink ribbon
- Fondant (page 128)
- Lemon extract
- Cornstarch for coating work surfaces

EQUIPMENT

- Cake boards: 6- and 8-inch (15 and 20 cm) heart-shaped separator boards
- Base: 14-inch (35 cm) foam-core base
- Icing tips: #3, #4, and #5 rounds; #104 petal; #24 closed star
- Cutters: lily cutter (for pink leaves)
- Icing bags and couplers
- Craft paintbrushes
- Plastic straws
- Toothpicks
- Rolling pin
- Metal spatulas
- Wax paper
- Scissors
- Turntable
- Electric mixer
- Bench scraper
- Icing smoother
- Hot glue gun

TIMING TIPS
• • •

The royal icing roses and gum-paste bow can be made anytime from two days to two weeks in advance. Since there are sixty roses and they need to be done in stages to allow the centers to dry, I'd recommend starting them a week in advance. Once they're completely dry, set them aside in a sealed container. The leaves on the bottom tier are attached to the cake while they are still pliable, so do not make them in advance. When the cakes are covered in fondant, give yourself an additional full day for painting; piping the filigree patterns, stems, and borders; and assembling the tiers.

TECHNIQUES YOU'LL USE

∎ ∎ ∎

Slicing, filling, and coating a cake
(page 22)

∎ ∎ ∎

Covering with fondant
(page 24)

∎ ∎ ∎

Building a tiered cake
(page 26)

∎ ∎ ∎

Piping techniques;
borders (page 29),
roses (page 31)

∎ ∎ ∎

Gum-paste decorations
(page 33)

∎ ∎ ∎

Painting with food color
(page 34)

∎ ∎ ∎

Using templates
(page 35)

IN ADVANCE
∎ ∎ ∎

1 Make the red royal icing roses. Let dry overnight. See Basic Instructions on page 29 for piping royal icing flowers. **2** Prepare the cake base: cover 14-inch (35 cm) base with pink flow-consistency royal icing and pipe pink royal icing bead border. Let dry for at least twenty-four hours. **3** Attach $\frac{1}{4}$-inch (6mm) ribbon to edge of the foam core base with a hot glue gun.

4. Bake and cool cakes completely.

5. Attach cakes to cake boards. Chill, fill, and apply crumb coat.

6. Set on base. Center and attach the 12-inch (30 cm) tier to the covered foam-core base with royal icing.

7. Cover the cakes with fondant. Let fondant set.

8. Paint the red tiers. In a small glass or ceramic bowl, mix red powdered food color with lemon extract to create a thin, syruplike consistency. To create the velvety texture, dip a clean sponge in the food color and then sponge-paint the heart-shaped tiers, the 12-inch (30 cm) tier, and just the top of the 10-inch (25 cm) tier with the red mixture. Once it's dry, give it another coat to build up the texture.

9. Paint the sides of the 10-inch (25 cm) tier pink. In a small glass or ceramic bowl, mix the pink powdered food color with lemon extract to create a thicker syruplike consistency. To create the suede-like texture, use a medium-sized flat craft brush and dab the color on in thick strokes. Once it's dry, give it another coat to build up the texture.

10. Pipe the filigree patterns around the sides of the heart-shaped tiers in pink royal icing using the #3 round decorating tip.

11. Paint the filigree patterns. Using a small to medium round craft brush, paint the filigree pattern on the smaller heart with a mixture of gold iridescent powder and lemon extract. Then paint the filigree pattern on the larger heart with a mixture of pink luster dust and lemon extract (see B, opposite).

12. Attach the roses to the clefts of the heart-shaped tiers with royal icing.

13. Mix pink paste food color into a small amount of gum paste. Cut out leaves with lily cutter (see A, opposite). Let dry.

14. Using the leaf-pattern templates as guides, attach the leaves in four groups to the front, back, and sides of the 12-inch (30 cm) tier, and then pipe lines as stems between the leaves with the #4 round decorating tip.

15. Cut support straws to size and insert into the three larger tiers.

16. Center, stack, and attach the tiers to each other with icing.

17. Pipe the royal icing borders. Blend a small amount of pink paste food color into the royal icing. Start with the smaller heart, and using the #24 star decorating tip, pipe a zig zag border around the bottom of the tier.

18. For the 10-inch (25 cm) tier: Use the #5 round decorating tip to pipe a beaded border around the top and bottom of the tier.

19. For the 12-inch (30 cm) tier: Pipe a line border around the bottom of the tier with the #5 round tip.

20. Paint the bottom borders of the smallest and the largest tiers, and the stems, with a mixture of gold iridescent powder and lemon extract.

21. Attach the bow with a small dot of royal icing, and then place a toothpick just below where you'd like the bow to sit and press it into the cake so that it's hidden but extended enough to add a little extra support to hold up the bow (see D, opposite).

A | MAKE LEAF CUTOUTS

Roll out gum paste to $\frac{1}{16}$-inch (1.5 mm) thickness and cut leaves with lily cutter. Attach to cake while they are still pliable so that they will conform to shape of cake.

B | DETAIL OF FILIGREE PATTERNS

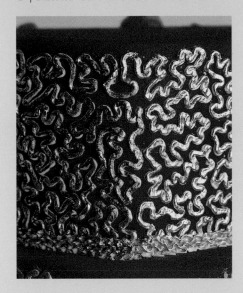

C | MAKE THE BOW

Roll out strings of pink gum paste to make loops, ends, and knots. Attach as shown with a few dabs of water.

D | DETAIL OF BOW

MONSOON WEDDING

MIRA NAIR'S *MONSOON WEDDING* IS ONE OF MY NEW FAVORITE MOVIES. RIGHT FROM THE OPENING CREDITS, I STARTED THINKING HOW WONDERFUL ITS COLORS AND SHAPES WERE. THE MOVIE SHOWCASES ALL THE MARVELOUS SIGHTS OF AN INDIAN WEDDING: HUNDREDS OF GARLANDS OF ORANGE AND GOLD MARIGOLDS, SARIS OF BEAUTIFULLY PATTERNED MULTIHUED FABRICS, SHINING FESTIVE JEWELRY. I WANTED TO MAKE A CAKE THAT REFLECTED THIS SPLENDOR—SUMPTUOUS ON THE OUTSIDE, CHOCOLATY RICH WITHIN.

CAKE

- 7-inch (18 cm) round tier, 3 inches (8 cm) high
- 10-inch (25 cm) round tier, 3 inches (8 cm) high
- 15-inch (35 cm) petal-shaped tier, 4 inches (10 cm) high

DECORATIONS

- 26 golden yellow royal icing chrysanthemums (always make extra)
- 40 orange royal icing chrysanthemums
- Royal icing (page 127)
- Dragées: small (3 mm), medium (4 mm), and large (5 mm) silver balls; silver oval dragées; and flat round dragées
- Gum-paste decorations: 5 bellflowers, 8 leaf cutouts
- Paste food color: sky blue, buttercup yellow, red, and orange
- Powdered food color: lime shimmer, gold, and deep pink luster dust
- Lemon extract
- Fondant (page 128)
- Cornstarch (for coating work surfaces)
- Ribbon: 1 $\frac{1}{2}$ yards (1.4 m) of $\frac{1}{2}$-inch (1 cm) pink ribbon

EQUIPMENT

- Cake boards: 7-, 10-, and 15-inch (18, 25, and 38 cm) round separator boards
- Base: 16-inch (40 cm) silver foil-covered foam-core
- Icing tips: #3 round; #80 and #81 specialty decorating tips
- Icing bags and couplers
- Flower nail
- 3-inch (8 cm) clear plastic pillars
- 6-inch (15 cm) clear plastic cake separators
- Cloth-covered wire: #22 gauge
- Wire cutter
- Florist's tape: white
- Trumpet flower tool
- Cutters: leaf, calyx
- Crepe paper
- Craft paintbrushes
- Plastic straws
- Toothpicks
- Rolling pin
- Metal spatulas
- Wax paper
- Scissors
- Turntable
- Electric mixer
- Bench scraper
- Icing smoother
- Hot glue gun

TIMING TIPS
• • •

The royal icing flowers should be made at least two days and up to two weeks in advance so that they'll have time to set. That will also give you time to assemble the garland swags and dry the icing that binds them to the wires. Leave at least twelve hours for the pink gum-paste leaves to dry.

Once the cakes are all baked, filled, and covered in fondant and icing flowers, I'd estimate a minimum of an additional full day for painting the shimmery bottom tier, creating the icing and dragée patterns and border, and assembling the tiers.

TECHNIQUES YOU'LL USE
• • •

Slicing, filling, and coating a cake
(page 22)

• • •

Covering with fondant
(page 24)

• • •

Building a tiered cake
(page 26)

• • •

Piping techniques
(page 29)

• • •

Chrysanthemum borders
(page 32)

• • •

Gum-paste decorations
(page 33)

• • •

Painting with food color
(page 34)

IN ADVANCE

■ ■ ■

1 **Make the royal icing chrysanthemums** (see Basic Instructions on page 32 for piping icing flowers) and let dry overnight. Use the #80 specialty tip for the larger golden flowers and the #81 for the smaller orange flowers. Reserve some of the yellow and orange royal icing for later, for attaching the flowers and filling in gaps on top tier. **2** Assemble the garland swags (see A, B, and C, opposite). **3** Cut out the gum-paste leaves for bottom of cake with leaf (or sunflower) cutter. Press the leaves into a small piece of crepe paper to create a textured surface, and pinch the pointed ends together. Let dry on paper towels or foam pad. **4** Paint the leaves with pink luster dust. **5** **Make the gum-paste bellflowers** (see D, opposite). **6** Paint the flowers with gold luster dust. With royal icing, attach a large dragée to the center of each flower as a stamen. **7** Attach the ribbon to the edge of foam core base of cake with a hot glue gun. **8** Place the 15-inch (38 cm) petal cake pan on top of the 15-inch (38 cm) round board and copy the bottom outline of the pan onto the board with a pencil. Cut to shape.

9. Bake and cool cakes completely.

10. Attach the cakes to their cake boards. Chill, fill, and apply crumb coat.

11. Center and attach the 15-inch (38 cm) tier to the foam-core base with royal icing.

12. Color the fondant. Blend buttercup yellow paste food color into the fondant for the top tier. Add just a little bit of red to make the color more golden. Wrap in plastic and set aside. Blend blue paste food color into the fondant for the center tier. (The fondant for the bottom tier will be left white and then painted later.)

13. Cover the cakes with fondant.

14. Pipe the diamond patterns onto the blue tier. Using the #3 round decorating tip, pipe blue royal icing patterns. The pattern consists of small royal icing crosses with a small dragée in the center of each cross, and small dots and large pill dragées in the centers of the diamonds (see E, opposite).

15. Start by piping the little cross shapes about 1 inch (2.5 cm) apart along the front top border of the blue tier. Then, work the pattern vertically from each cross. For example, in the center row of the photo, I've made a second cross just below the first one and in the center of the tier, and a third one just below that at the bottom of the tier.

16. Working from the next little cross shape down, attach a large pill dragée, then a cross shape, then a dragée, and a cross again. To complete the diamond pattern in that row, pipe the crosses on either side of the large dragée and then pipe a small blue dot diagonally between each of the crosses.

17. In a small glass or ceramic bowl, mix lime shimmer luster dust with lemon extract. Paint the petal-shaped tier in smooth, even strokes. Once it's dry, you can give it another coat if you feel it needs it.

18. Attach the chrysanthemums to the 7-inch (18 cm) tier with royal icing. Fill in any gaps between flowers with additional petals using the #80 specialty decorating tip.

19. Insert the support straws. Cut the straws to size and insert into the two largest tiers.

20. Center, stack, and attach the blue tier to the petal tier with icing. (If the cake is traveling, do not put the top tier and garlands on until you arrive; they won't survive the trip unless they're packed properly.)

21. Position the clear plastic columns fitted and snapped into the separator plates. Center and attach on top of the blue tier with royal icing. Place and attach the cake board with the garland on top of the top plastic divider. Bend the wire so that the garlands hang down.

22. Center, stack, and attach the 7-inch (18 cm) tier to the top of the plastic columns fitted with the plastic separator plates, using royal icing.

23. Insert the bellflower wires into the bottom of the chrysanthemum-covered top tier so that they hang at the points between where the garlands meet.

24. Add the icing and dragée borders. Attach along the bottoms of the chrysanthemum and petal tiers using the #3 round decorating tip. For the chrysanthemum tier border, affix a continuous beaded border of small dragées with royal icing. For the blue tier's border, attach one row of small dragées around the bottom edge of the cake and add an outer row of oval dragées pointing outward at every tenth dragée in the previous row.

25. Add little dragée flowers to the top edge of the petal tier between each petal with royal icing. The flowers are made up of 4 mm dragée centers circled by six 3 mm dragées.

26. Attach the pink leaves to the base of cake between each petal. Attach a 5 mm dragée where the petal meets the cake, and a small one in the center of the leaf.

A | ASSEMBLE THE GARLANDS

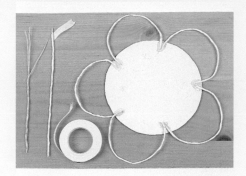

Cut cloth-covered wire into five 9-inch (23 cm) sections. Cover in white florist's tape. (The wire should be sturdy, so use a heavy gauge, or if you use a thin gauge, double or triple it up, then wrap in florist's tape). Form U shapes with wires. Use a hot glue gun to attach wires to 7-inch (18 cm) cake board. Space them 4 inches (10 cm) apart. Each glued end should overlap the board by $\frac{3}{4}$ inch (2 cm).

B | ATTACH FLOWERS TO GARLANDS

Place a thin cushion of paper towels or bubble wrap under one of the wires and attach four orange chrysanthemums facedown on the bottom of the wire and then four chrysanthemums faceup, using orange royal icing. Repeat for all five wires. Let dry completely.

C | FINISH THE GARLANDS

When you're ready to put the garlands on the cake, attach cake border to top of clear plastic separator plates and columns with royal icing, and fold wires downward.

D | TO FORM A BELLFLOWER

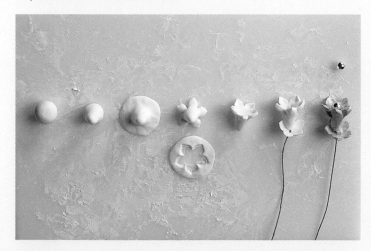

Roll a small ball of gum paste into a cone. Flatten the bottom edge to form a brim. Use small calyx cutter to cut. Hollow out center with trumpet tool, and use a ball tool to give petals curved shape. Moisten hooked end of a medium-gauge wire wrapped in florist tape and insert into flower. Place thin calyx onto wire and attach to bellflower with water.

E | DETAIL OF BEADWORK ON BLUE TIER

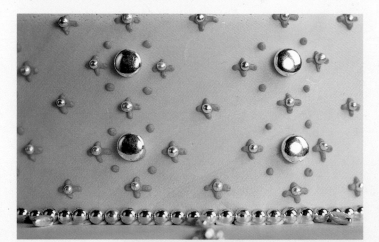

F | DETAIL OF GARLAND

BICYCLE BUILT FOR TWO

WE FOUND THIS WHIMSICAL METAL COUPLE DURING A ROMANTIC TRIP TO PARIS. I ADMIRED IT SO MUCH THAT THE SHOPKEEPER GAVE IT TO US, WITH A NOD AND A WINK. AT THE TIME, DAVID WAS A LITTLE MORTIFIED—AT THAT POINT, MARRIAGE WASN'T EVEN ON HIS RADAR SCREEN. BUT HE CAME AROUND, AND THESE BICYCLERS ARE STILL WITH US. I WANTED TO CREATE A SOFT CAROUSEL EFFECT FOR THEM AND THEIR DOG, WITH SHADES OF YELLOW FONDANT AND WHITE ICING STRIPES, SWAGS, AND BOWS. THE SCALLOPED TIER IS BASED ON THE AWNING OF PETIT ABEILLE, OUR FAVORITE NEW YORK BREAKFAST PLACE. AND, OF COURSE, I HAD TO ADD SOME EIFFEL TOWERS.

TIMING TIPS

· · ·

The royal icing Eiffel Towers and bows should be made at least twenty-four hours and up to two weeks in advance. As for the gum-paste decorations, the moons (circles) should have about twelve hours to dry. The scalloped edge is the exception to the rule, it needs to be attached to the cake while it's still pliable, so roll it out when you're ready to attach it; do not make it in advance.

There's a fair amount of detail to be piped onto this cake after the fondant is put on, so allow at least a full day for painting, piping, and assembling the tiers.

CAKES

- 4-inch (10 cm) round tier, 3 (8 cm) inches high
- 5-inch (13- cm) round tier, 3 (8 cm) inches high
- 7-inch (18 cm) round tier, 3 (8 cm) inches high
- 9-inch (23 cm) round tier, 3 (8 cm) inches high

DECORATIONS

- Royal icing (page 127)
- 5 royal icing string bows
- Fondant (page 128)
- 9 royal icing Eiffel Towers (page 135)
- Dragées: small (3 mm) silver dragées
- Gum-paste decorations: nine 1-inch (2.5 cm) circles; scalloped edge
- Paste food color: yellow

- Powdered food color: silver shimmer luster dust; royal blue, buttercup yellow, and white petal dust; white sparkle dust
- Lemon extract
- Cornstarch for coating work surface
- Bride-and-groom cake topper
- Ribbon: 2 yards (1.8 m) of $\frac{1}{4}$ -inch (6 mm) blue velvet ribbon

EQUIPMENT

- Cake boards: 4-, 5-, 7-, and 9-inch (10, 13, 18, and 23 cm) round separator boards
- Base: 10-inch (25 cm) fondant-covered foam-core
- Plastic dowel rods
- 4-inch (10 cm) plastic separator plate
- Icing tips: #2, #3, #5, and #6 round; #44 basket-weave

- Icing bags and couplers
- Cutters: 1- and 2-inch (2.5 and 5 cm) circles
- Serrated knife
- Craft knife
- 90-degree triangle
- Tracing wheel
- Craft paintbrushes
- Plastic straws
- Toothpicks
- Rolling pin
- Metal spatulas
- Wax paper
- Scissors
- Turntable
- Electric mixer
- Bench scraper
- Icing smoother
- Hot glue gun

IN ADVANCE

• • •

1 **Make the royal icing Eiffel Towers** (see A, B, and C, opposite) and let dry overnight. (These are very fragile. Always make extra royal icing decorations.) **2** Pipe royal icing bows. Let dry overnight. **3** Using a #3 decorating tip, pipe five 2-inch (5 cm) figure-eight shaped bows on to wax paper. Let set for an hour or two and pipe a second layer of icing over the bows to reinforce. Place a dragee in the center of each bow. **4** Make 1-inch (2.5 cm) circle cutouts and let set. Coat the circles with a dusting of silver shimmer luster dust. **5** Prepare the cake base: Cover the 10-inch (25 cm) base, including the edge, with white fondant. Let set for at least twenty-four hours. Paint the edge of the base with a mixture of royal blue petal dust and lemon extract. Attach $\frac{1}{4}$-inch (6mm) ribbon to the edge of the foam core base with a hot glue gun.

6. Bake and cool cakes completely.

7. Attach cakes to the cake boards. Chill, fill, and apply crumb coat.

8. **Color the fondant.** Blend a touch of yellow paste food color into the fondant to make it a very pale yellow color.

9. Cover the cakes with fondant. First, cover the smallest tier with the very pale yellow fondant. Blend a little bit more yellow paste food color into the balance of the fondant to make a shade slightly darker for the 5-inch (13 cm) tier, and cover with fondant. Continue adding just a touch more color for each tier so that the tone gradually becomes more yellow from the top down. Cover the 7- and 9-inch (18 and 23 cm) tiers with fondant.

10. **Create guidelines for piping** royal icing. For the smallest tier, while the fondant is still soft, gently trace the stripes and swags. Use the 2-inch (5 cm) circle cutter to make light indentations for the swags. Line up the triangle with the bottom of the tier and, using the tracing wheel, make vertical guidelines under where each bow will be and from the bottom center of each swag to the bottom of the tier (see D, opposite).

11. For the 5-inch (15 cm) tier, use a ribbon or piece of paper as a guide to form the horizontal lines in the center of the tier with the tracing wheel.

12. For the 7-inch (18 cm) tier, line up the triangle with the bottom of the tier to make a series of vertical guidelines approximately $\frac{3}{8}$ inch (1 cm) apart.

13. **Paint the stripes and swags.** Mix buttercup yellow in equal parts with white powdered food color and add lemon extract. For the smallest tier, paint every other thick stripe a shade darker than the fondant. Paint the half circle inside the swags a shade darker than the stripes. Paint the top of the cake with white sparkle dust.

14. For the 5-inch (13 cm) tier, paint the horizontal stripe in the center a shade darker than the fondant.

15. **Insert plastic dowel rods** to float the 7-inch (18 cm) tier above the 9-inch (23 cm) tier. Start by centering the 4-inch (10 cm) separator plate on top of the 9-inch (23 cm) tier. Gently press the plate into the fondant to score an X where each dowel will be inserted.

16. Insert a dowel over one of the marks as straight as possible into the cake. Mark the dowel one inch above the top of the cake. (From the bottom of the dowel to where you've marked it will be approximately 4 to 4 $\frac{1}{4}$ inches (10 to 11 cm) when you take it out of the cake.)

17. Using that dowel as a guide, cut all four dowels with a serrated knife to the same length so that when they are inserted into the cake you will have 1-inch (2.5 cm) columns to suspend the 7-inch (18 cm) tier on.

18. Cut support straws to size and insert into the 7-inch (18 cm) tier.

19. Place the 4-inch (10 cm) separator plate on top of the dowels and snap into position, and attach the 7-inch (18 cm) tier on top of it with royal icing.

20. **Make the scallop edging.** Roll out a strip of gum paste to about $\frac{1}{16}$ inch (1.5 mm) thick and place the scallop template on top of it. Use a craft knife to cut out the scallop shape. You'll need four of these scalloped strips to cover the circumference of the tier. Attach the scallop strips to the tier with a small amount of water so that the top edge of the strip is about 1 inch (2.5 cm) from the bottom of the 7-inch (18 cm) tier and the ends of the strips meet.

21. Cut support straws to size and insert into the 5-inch (13 cm) tier.

22. Center, stack, and attach the 4- and 5-inch (10 and 13 cm) tiers to each other.

23. **Pipe royal icing decorations onto the cake.** For the smallest tier, pipe lines of

A | MAKE THE BASES OF THE EIFFEL TOWERS

Trace just the outline of the Eiffel Tower template in royal icing with the #3 round decorating tip. Let dry.

B | BUILD UPON BASES

Pipe second line of royal icing filling in squiggly inside lines of the template. Let dry.

C | COMPLETE THE TOWERS

Pipe a third layer of icing to reinforce the tower. These will be the exact same outlines done in the first step, with the addition of a vertical line down the center of each tower leg and three very short vertical lines in the arch.

dots with the #3 round decorating tip following along the guidelines. With the #6 round decorating tip, pipe a border of hearts (running sideways) along the top edge of cake and a small curlicue in the corners of each swag. Pipe a fat dot of icing where the bow will be placed and let dry, this will give the bow something to sit on so that it doesn't just lie flat against the side of the cake. Once these support dots dry, attach the bows with royal icing. Pipe a dot border around the bottom of the tier with the #5 round decorating tip, and then pipe smaller dots with the #3 tip between each dot.

24. For the 5-inch (13 cm) tier, alternate dots made with the #5 round decorating tip with dot flowers made with the #3 round decorating tip along the outlines of the horizontal yellow stripe. Place a small dragée in the center of each flower. Pipe hearts along the top edge in about the same position the bows are on the tier above. Finish off with dot border after all tiers are stacked.

25. For the 7-inch (18 cm) tier, The stripes are a repeated pattern as follows:

a single stripe of dots made with the #5 round decorating tip; then three skinny stripes made with the #2 tip that fit inside the next pair of guidelines; a ribbon made with the #44 basket-weave tip that fits inside the next pair of guidelines with tiny dot borders running down both sides made with the #2 tip; another set of three skinny stripes; then another single line of #5 dots. (It sounds more complicated than it is; use the photos for reference.)

26. For the largest tier, pipe a beaded border along the bottom of the cake using the #6 round decorating tip.

27. Center and attach them to the 7-inch (18 cm) tier with icing. (If the cake is being transported, do this step on site.)

28. **Attach cycling bride-and-groom** cake topper with a few dabs of royal icing.

29. Attach the very fragile Eiffel Towers and circles last. Place the towers around the largest tier more or less equidistant from each other. Attach the circles with a dab of water toward the top edge of the tier between each tower (see E, opposite). Voila!

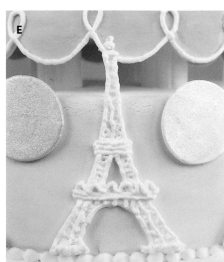

CASABLANCA CAKE

TIMING TIPS

• • •

This is a complicated cake with several stages of production. The fondant spire should be made at least twenty-four hours and up to two weeks in advance. Since the silver tier is carved, it's important that the cake layers are well chilled and sturdy before you begin to put them together. I recommend baking at least three days in advance to give the cakes a full day to chill. There's also a lot of detail to be piped onto this cake after the fondant is put on, so allow extra time for painting, piping, and assembling the tiers.

WHEN *MODERN BRIDE* MAGAZINE ASKED ME TO DESIGN A CAKE FOR A STORY ON A MOROCCAN-THEMED WEDDING, I KNEW I HAD TO DO A LITTLE HOMEWORK. I GOT A SENSE OF THE COLORS AND PATTERNS FROM GUIDEBOOKS, AND CHOSE COBALT BLUE AND SILVER TO COMPLEMENT THE RICH ORANGE AND RED TONES IN MOROCCAN TEXTILES. THE HENNA HAND-PAINTING DESIGNS ALONG THE BLUE TIERS WERE SUGGESTED BY TRADITIONAL MOROCCAN MOTIFS, AND THE SHINY CURVED SILVER TIER IS BASED ON A TEAPOT I SAW IN A GUIDEBOOK. THE MOST ENJOYABLE RESEARCH OF ALL WAS SITTING BACK TO WATCH A DVD OF *CASABLANCA*. THE SPIRE THAT TOPS THE CAKE COMES FROM THAT CLASSIC 1942 FILM.

CAKE

- 9-inch (23 cm) round tier, 3 inches (8 cm) high
- 10-inch (25 cm) round tier, 3 inches (8 cm) high
- 15-inch (38 cm) hexagonal tier, 4 inches (10 cm) high

DECORATIONS

- Fondant spire
- Gum-paste decorations: 2 circles
- Powdered food color: silver highlighter, white sparkle luster dust, silver iridescent powder, turquoise petal dust
- Food color marker: fine blue line
- Lemon extract
- Dragées: flat round
- Royal icing (page 127)

- Cornstarch for coating work surfaces
- Fondant (page 128)
- Ribbon: 1 ½ yards (1.4 m) of ½-inch (13 mm) light blue satin ribbon

EQUIPMENT

- Cake boards: 7-, 9-, 10-, and 15-inch (18, 23, 25, and 38 cm) round
- Base: 14-inch (36 cm) silver foil-covered foam-core base
- Styrofoam ball: 3 inches (8 cm) (for spire)
- Icing tips: #2, #3, and #5 round decorating tips
- Icing bags and couplers
- Gum-paste cutters: 1- and 2-inch (2.5 and 5 cm) circles
- Craft paint brushes
- Triangle
- Tracing wheel

- Templates (pages 136–137)
- Cloth-covered wire: #22 gauge
- Florist's tape: white
- Wax paper
- Scissors
- Serrated knife
- Turntable
- Skewers
- Wooden dowels
- Toothpicks
- Plastic straws
- Rolling pin
- Metal spatula
- Electric mixer
- Bench scraper
- Icing smoother
- Hot glue gun

IN ADVANCE
...

1 Make circle cutouts for the top of the spire and let set. Paint the circles with a mixture of silver highlighter and white sparkle luster dust and lemon extract. Attach the circles, small one on top and 1 inch (2.5 cm) apart, to the blunt end of a skewer with royal icing. Let set. **2 Make the spire** (see A, B, and C opposite). **3** Insert the circles attached to the skewer into top of spire. **4 Make the swirl handles** for either side of the spire. Take 18 inches (45 cm) of cloth-covered wire and wrap in florist's tape. Bend into swirl shapes. The bottom halves of the cake will be bent later to conform to the shape of the silver tier. Set aside. **5** Place the hexagonal cake pan on top of the 15-inch (38 cm) round cake board and copy the bottom outline of the pan onto the board with a pencil. Cut to shape.

6. Bake and cool cakes completely.

7. Attach the 10- and 15-inch (25 and 38 cm) tiers to their cake boards. Chill, fill, and apply crumb coat.

8. Place the 9-inch (23 cm) tier on its board, but don't attach. Chill and fill the tier (do not apply crumb coat yet).

9. Carve the 9-inch (23 cm) tier, use a serrated knife to round out the top and bottom edges, to form a shape a little like a flying saucer. Attach the tier to the 7-inch (18 cm) board and apply crumb coat.

10. Cover the tiers in fondant.

11. **Trace the template designs.** While the fondant is still pliable, use a straight pin to trace the templates (pages 136–137) for the patterns on the sides of the 10- and 15-inch (25 and 38 cm) tiers.

12. Create guidelines for the grid patterns on the sides of the hexagonal tier. Use a tracing wheel to score a checkered pattern with $1\frac{1}{2}$-inch (3 cm) squares. To make the vertical lines, align the bottom edge of the triangle with the bottom edge of the cake and emboss equidistant vertical lines along the vertical edge of the triangle. For the horizontal lines, run the tracing wheel along the bottom edge of the triangle, using the vertical lines to line up the triangle. Let fondant set.

13. **Paint backgrounds** of the two bottom tiers using a mixture of turquoise powdered food color and lemon extract. Use a medium craft brush and paint with smooth, even strokes. Once it's dry, give it another coat to build up the density.

14. Copy and cut out the grid stencils (pages 136–137), and using the guides you've just drawn, trace the bracelike shapes with a blue fine-line food color marker.

15. **Pipe the royal icing designs** onto the cakes. For the blue tiers, pipe lines of icing with the #3 round decorating tip following along the guidelines. Let set.

16. For the silver tier, pipe five rows of dots with the #5 round decorating tip around the circumference of the tier. Let set.

17. Paint the 9-inch (23 cm) tier. Mix silver iridescent powdered food color with lemon extract to syrup consistency and paint the tier in smooth, even strokes. Repeat. Let dry.

18. Cut support straws to size and insert them into the blue tiers.

19. **Stack the tiers.** Center, stack, and attach the tiers to each other with icing. When handling the silver tier, the color will come off on your hands, so be careful not to touch the other tiers until you wash the silver off your hands.

20. Paint the royal icing designs on the blue tiers. Mix equal parts of silver highlighter and white sparkle luster dust with a small amount of lemon extract, and paint the designs using a small round paintbrush. Let dry. (See D, opposite.)

21. **Attach the spire.** Cut three support straws to size and insert in a small circle in the center of the silver tier under where the spire will sit. Pipe a small circle of royal icing to hold the topper in place. Insert the dowel that the spire is on into

the center of the tier and set in position with royal icing. Affix the dragées in a border around the spire. Let set.

22. Attach the wire handles. Bend the bottoms of the wires to conform to the shape of the cake. Use a few straight pins to temporarily tack them into place (until icing sets); attach to the sides of the cake with dots of royal icing using the #5 round tip.

23. Pipe small dots of royal icing to the sides of the swirls with the #3 tip. (This cannot be done in advance because they pop off when you bend and handle the wires.)

24. **Pipe the royal icing borders.** For the 10- and 15-inch (25 and 38 cm) tiers: use the #3 round decorating tip to pipe beaded borders around the bottom of both tiers. Use the #2 round decorating tip to pipe beaded borders around the top edge and down the corner edges of the hexagonal tier.

25. Paint over the icing dots and borders and the wires with silver iridescent powder mixed with lemon extract.

TECHNIQUES YOU'LL USE
...

A | MAKE SPIRE TOPPER

B | MOLD POINT AND SPIRALS

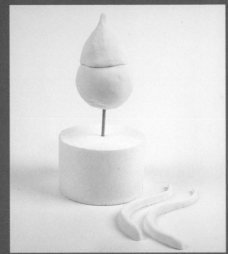

C | COMPLETE TOPPER

Start by covering the Styrofoam ball with fondant for base of spire. Insert wooden dowel about halfway into ball. (Shown inserted into a temporary cake dummy as temporary support.)

Shape a pointed cap from the fondant and attach to the ball with a few drops of water. Let set overnight. Make tapered 8-inch (20 cm) sausages of fondant one at a time and sculpt into a spiral shape. Attach to spire shape with a small amount of water while they are still pliable.

Continue adding the tapered spirals around the spire. Let set. Mix equal parts of silver highlighter and white sparkle luster dust with a small amount of lemon extract and paint the spire. Let dry and paint a second coat.

D | DETAILS OF ICING PATTERNS

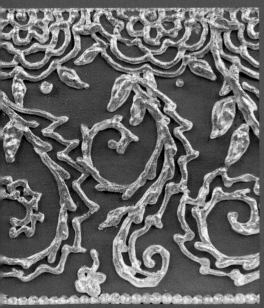

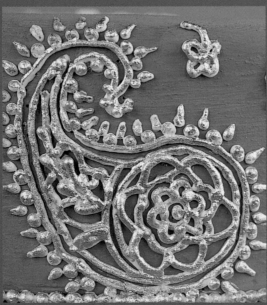

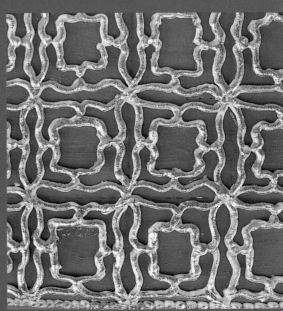

CAKE TOPPERS

■ ■ ■

As old-fashioned as bride-and-groom cake toppers may seem, they deserve a second look. They don't have to look clichéd. The right topper can put a great finishing touch on a cake, inspiring a creative, funny, or romantic feel.

The bicycle cake topper (opposite) imparts a sense of spontaneity because the figures are in motion. They have the quality of an illustration come to life. The Jackpot cake topper (opposite) has a fun, whimsical twist; the groom sweeping the bride off her feet. He's looking at her with an interesting mix of excitement and fear... which pretty much sums up the moment for a lot of grooms. The Philadelphia Story cake topper (page 89) has a timelessly stylish feel. I painted it and added decoration to the bride's hair, to give her a Katherine Hepburn, movie-star quality.

The thing that makes many of these pieces unique is that they're not intended to be cake toppers at all. In some cases, companies that specialize in figurines happen to have one or two brides and grooms in their product line. For example, a model railroad supplier makes the Jackpot and hat-doffing figures.

Another great way to find interesting and out-of-the-ordinary cake toppers is to scour antiques shops, online auctions, or even family closets for vintage brides and grooms.

They can be really special, and if they're a little distressed and you're up for giving them a facelift, you can usually get them for a steal.

HAND-HOLDING TOPPER	**KEWPIE-DOLL TOPPER**	**HAT-DOFFING TOPPER**
■ ■ ■	■ ■ ■	■ ■ ■

HAND-HOLDING TOPPER

■ ■ ■

I love this whimsical stylized bride and groom looking straight ahead and somewhat vulnerable. They're made by a Paris-based company called Pixi & Cie (see Sources, page 141).

2 $\frac{1}{4}$ inches (6 cm) tall.

KEWPIE-DOLL TOPPER

■ ■ ■

Okay, the groom isn't wearing any pants—you gotta love that! Similar versions are available through online auctions or antique shops.

2 $\frac{1}{2}$ inches (6.5 cm) tall.

HAT-DOFFING TOPPER

■ ■ ■

The bride and groom are totally animated and on their way to their new life together. Made by Preiser, a maker of model railroad supplies and figurines and sold by Walthers Model Railroad supplies (see Sources, page 141).

3 $\frac{1}{2}$ inches (9 cm) tall.

CENTERPIECE CAKES

· · · ·

An alternative to one big wedding cake is a series of small cakes
used as centerpieces. For one thing, you can have a number of
different themes. Another nice side effect is that people tend to
visit other tables a bit more so that they can see all the cakes.
At our wedding, every other table had either a flower centerpiece
or a cake centerpiece, and it was a great icebreaker.

3-D Cakes

Before I started making them myself,

I'd always thought cakes all came in the iconic round shape our grand-mothers used to make. Now I find that mixing up the shapes of pans, even carving cakes to the shape I like, is a big part of the fun of cake making.

The structure is the important thing here. Once you've got your foundations and supports in place, the sky's the limit. The techniques used in stacking a vertical cake are basically the same as in stacking any tiered cake, but without tiers in graduated sizes, the cake seems to defy gravity.

The methods used in making the Cuppa Joe to Go (page 111) can be applied to making a box-shaped cake, a pyramid cake, or a castle cake. The 3-D Kitty Cake (page 114) uses the same techniques you would use to make a teddy bear or boat or any carved shape.

Some of the cakes featured in other chapters of the book use three-dimensional elements, such as the Ella Fant Dance cake (page 41), created with ball-shaped pans, or the carved teapot tier in the Casablanca Cake (page 102).

You can buy all sorts of wonderful preshaped pans, molded to create freestanding characters ranging from bunnies to favorite TV characters. You'll also find 3-D pans for shapes that lie flat, like a horseshoe or an open book.

CUPPA JOE TO GO

MAYBE IT SEEMS A LITTLE OBVIOUS, BUT WHEN A FRIEND OF MINE NAMED JOE WAS LEAVING FOR A NEW JOB, THIS CUPPA JOE TO GO CAKE SEEMED LIKE A FITTING FAREWELL. I THOUGHT I WAS BEING ORIGINAL, BUT SINCE THEN I'VE SEEN MANY VARIATIONS ON THIS THEME IN CAKE BOOKS: COFFEE CUPS, TEA CUPS, MUGS. THIS ONE HAS A LITTLE BIT OF AN IRONIC SPIN: GREEK DINERS ACROSS NEW YORK CITY ALL FEATURE THIS CLASSIC CUP, WHICH ALWAYS PROCLAIMS, "HAPPY TO SERVE YOU!"—EVEN IF THE GUYS AT THE COUNTER DON'T SEEM AT ALL HAPPY TO DO SO.

TIMING TIPS

• • •

As with any carved and/or tall vertical cake, you want it to be well chilled and sturdy. I recommend baking it three days in advance to give the layers a chance to set. Once it's covered in fondant, give yourself a full day for decorating, since all the decorations are painted or piped directly onto the cake, as opposed to being made in advance.

CAKE

- Two 6-inch (15 cm) round tiers, each 4 inches (10 cm) high

DECORATIONS

- Powdered food colors: blue, brown, and turquoise
- Paste food color: blue and brown
- Lemon extract
- Royal icing (page 127)
- Fondant (page 128)
- Cornstarch and shortening (for coating the work surfaces)

EQUIPMENT

- Cake boards: two 6-inch (15 cm) round
- Base: 8-inch (20 cm) silver foil-covered foam-core base
- Icing tips: #2, #3, and #5
- Icing bag and coupler
- Decoration templates (page 138)
- Serrated knife
- Rolling pin
- Turntable
- Plastic straws
- Craft paintbrushes
- Toothpicks
- Metal spatula
- Wax paper
- Scissors
- Electric mixer
- Bench scraper
- Icing smoother

TECHNIQUES YOU'LL USE

• • •

Slicing, filling, and coating a cake (page 22)

• • •

Covering with fondant (page 24)

• • •

Building a tiered cake (page 26)

• • •

Piping techniques (page 29)

• • •

Painting with food color (page 34)

• • •

Using templates (page 35)

2. Bake and cool cakes completely.

3. Set, but do not attach, the tiers onto cake boards for easier handling.

4. Fill layers and chill cakes.

5. Insert support straws cut to size into one of the tiers. We'll call this bottom tier, tier I.

6. Stack and assemble tiers. Center and attach the trimmed cake board (from step 1) with buttercream icing to the top of tier I.

7. Spread a layer of buttercream on top of the board, and center the second 6-inch (15 cm) tier, which will be the top of the cake (tier II), on top of that.

8. Form a center support by placing a straw or dowel vertically through the center of the cake.

9. Wrap loosely with plastic wrap and return to refrigerator for about three hours to let filling set.

10. Turn the cake upside-down so that tier I is temporarily on top. This makes it easier to carve it into the tapered shape of a cardboard coffee cup.

11. Carve the cake. Use a serrated knife to shape the cake into an upside-down to-go coffee cup. Trim about an inch all the way around the top of the cake and continue down at a slight outward angle toward the base. (See A, opposite.)

12. Center and attach the 8-inch (20 cm) foam-core base foil-side down to the top of the cake with icing.

13. Slide a spatula under the cake board below tier B to lift up. Place one hand underneath and the other on top and turn cake upside down so that the base is now on the bottom. Remove the 6-inch (15 cm) cake board from what is now the top of the cake.

14. Cover the cake with a crumb coat of buttercream.

15. Cover with fondant.

16. Trace the designs onto the cup. While the fondant is still pliable, use a straight pin to trace the templates (page 138) of the lettering and patterns on the front and back of the cup and the pitchers on the sides of the cup.

17. Paint the areas around the We Are Happy to Serve You plaque and the pitchers using a mixture of blue powdered food color and lemon extract. Leave about a ½-inch (13 mm) unpainted white border around the bottom of the cake.

18. Pipe double lines for the brown royal icing lettering using a #3 round decorating tip. Let dry completely before painting.

19. Pipe the white beaded border around the words using a #5 round decorating tip. Using the same tip, make the beaded scroll borders at the top and bottom of the cake.

20. Using the #2 round decorating tip, pipe the outlines for the pitchers and the designs inside in royal icing colored with blue paste food color. Let dry.

21. Paint the lettering and the top of the cake with a coffee brown combination of powdered food color and lemon extract.

22. Give the pitchers highlights by overpainting with some turquoise powdered food color mixed with lemon extract.

23. Make the rim of the cup (see B, opposite). Attach the rope rim with a little bit of water to make it sticky.

∎ ∎ ∎

A │ STACK AND CARVE THE TIERS

TIER I

TIER II

After supports have been placed in bottom tier and the tiers have been stacked on top of each other, this cake is turned upside-down. This makes it easier to carve into the tapered shape of a cardboard coffee cup.

B │ MAKE RIM OF CUP

Roll the fondant into a rope. Keep rolling and moving your hands apart until you have a length of 26 inches (65 cm). A light coating of vegetable shortening works better than corn-starch (shown in photo) for coating your hands and work surface for rolling a rope of fondant.

C │ SERVING SUGGESTION

WE ARE HAPPY TO SERVE YOU

Enjoy a hearty helping of your Cuppa Joe cake with a cup of the real thing.

3-D KITTY CAKE

I'M A BIG HELLO KITTY FAN, AND THIS CAKE IS A NOD TO THAT FUN KITSCH JAPANESE ANIME SENSIBILITY THAT KITTY EMBODIES. THE CAKE WAS MADE IN HONOR OF MY FRIEND GABRIELLE, WHO HAS QUITE AN AMAZING SENSIBILITY HERSELF. ONE STEP INTO GABRIELLE'S HOME AND YOU CAN SEE THAT PINK IS HER VERY FAVORITE COLOR, AND SO HAD TO BE THE OVERALL COLOR SCHEME OF HER CAKE. THE TEXTURE ALSO HAD TO BE PLUSH, WARM, AND COZY TO MATCH HER LOVING SPIRIT.

CAKES

- 5-inch (13 cm) round tier, 3 inches (8 cm) high
- 8-inch (20 cm) square, 2 inches (5 cm) high
- 3 halves of 6-inch (15 cm) ball cakes

DECORATIONS

- Buttercream icing (page 126)
- Royal icing (page 127)
- Fondant (page 128)
- Powdered food color: red, black, and yellow petal dust; super red luster dust
- Paste food color: pink
- Lemon extract
- Cornstarch (for coating fondant work surface)
- Toothpicks

EQUIPMENT

- Cake boards: two 5-inch (13 cm) round, three 6-inch (15 cm) round, and one 8-inch (20 cm) square
- Cake templates (page 139) for ears, arms, and legs
- Decoration templates (page 139) for face and bow
- Base: two 12-inch (30 cm) heart-shaped boards
- Icing tips: #3, #5, and #10
- Icing bags and couplers
- Craft paintbrushes
- Skewers
- Rolling pin
- Electric mixer
- Turntable
- Plastic straws
- Metal spatula
- Wax paper
- Plastic wrap
- Ruler
- Scissors
- Hot glue gun
- Bench scraper

TIMING TIPS

• • •

Since this is a very vertical cake and Hello Kitty's head happens to be bigger than her body, it's important that the cake layers are well chilled and sturdy before you begin to put them together. I recommend baking at least three days in advance to give the cakes a full day to chill and to allow a full day to decorate. The fondant-covered heart base, fondant bow, and royal icing eyes and nose can be made up to two weeks in advance. The fondant for the face needs to be rolled out just before you're ready to apply it so it can conform to the shape of the head. Ice the legs separately and attach them last, after icing the rest of the body. Otherwise it is difficult to get to the inside areas.

IN ADVANCE

. . .

1 Prepare the base by gluing together two 12-inch (30 cm) hearts and covering with fondant. Paint the fondant heart with two coats of red petal dust mixed with lemon extract. **2 Make the fondant bow** (see A, opposite). **3** Pipe the royal icing eyes and nose using templates (page 139). When dry, paint the eyes black, the nose yellow, and the bow super red (which looks like a shiny bright pink) with a mixture of powdered food coloring and lemon extract. NOTE: The black powder will get on your hands even after it dries, so be very careful when handling.

TECHNIQUES YOU'LL USE

. . . .

Slicing, filling, and coating a cake
(page 22)

. . . .

Covering with fondant
(page 24)

. . . .

Building a tiered cake
(page 26)

. . . .

Piping techniques
(page 29)

. . . .

Painting with food color
(page 34)

. . . .

Using templates
(page 35)

---

4. Bake and cool cakes completely.

5. Fill the 5-inch (13 cm) tier and attach it to the 5-inch (13 cm) cake board. (You can, but it's not necessary to crumb coat this cake).

6. Insert support straws into the 5-inch (13 cm) tier and cut to size (see B, opposite).

7. Set, but do not attach, the square and half-circle tiers onto the cake boards for easier handling, and chill all the cakes well.

8. Using the templates (page 139), cut arms, legs, and ears from the square tier.

9. Trim 1 inch (2.5 cm) off the top of the round ends of two of the three half-circle cakes to form small flat surfaces. (Leave the last half circle completely round because that will be the top of the head.)

10. Stack and assemble tiers (see C, opposite). Start with the 5-inch (13 cm) tier and cover the top with buttercream. Cut a 1-inch (2.5 cm) hole into the center of a 5-inch (13 cm) cake board and place it on top of the 5-inch (13 cm) tier. Form a center support by placing three skewers through the hole and the center of the cake.

11. Place one of the trimmed half balls with the wide, flat side down through the skewers and on top of the 5-inch (13 cm) tier to form chest and shoulders. Carve to match the width of the 5-inch (13 cm) tier.

12. Place the second trimmed half ball with the wide, flat side up through skewers and on top of the first. Place the last half ball flat side down to form the top of the head.

13. Attach the ears with toothpicks and the arms with skewers cut to size, 3 to 5 inches (8 to 13 cm) as needed (see D, opposite). The legs will be attached after you ice the rest of the cake.

14. Wrap the cake sculpture loosely with plastic wrap and return to the refrigerator for at least three hours.

15. When the cake is chilled, attach bottom cake (with board) to the fondant-covered heart base.

16. Give Kitty her face. Roll out a fairly thick layer of fondant, about $\frac{1}{4}$ inch (6 mm) thick, and cut out an oval for the face. Apply a coat of thinned buttercream to where the face will be positioned and gently attach the fondant oval to the face.

17. Cover the body with a chenillelike snowsuit. Mix a small amount of pink

paste food color into buttercream icing until you have a pink you like. Use a #10 round decorating tip and, starting around the oval of the face, pipe balls of buttercream in rows to cover the entire head (except for the fondant face), body, and arms.

18. Position the legs so they are touching the front of the body and are approximately $1\frac{1}{2}$ inches (4 cm) apart from each other. Pipe balls of icing to cover the legs and feet. Build up two or three extra rows of balls on the front top edge of the legs to form toes.

19. Attach the eyes and nose with royal icing, taking special care not to smudge the powdered color onto the fondant. Attach the bow with toothpicks.

20. Insert three toothpicks on either side of the face to form whiskers and use a #5 round decorating tip to pipe royal icing to cover the toothpicks. When the icing is dry, paint it with a mixture of black petal dust and lemon extract.

21. Remember to remove the toothpicks and skewers before serving the cake.

A | MAKE KITTY'S BOW

Use the template to form the center ball and two tear-shaped sides. Press your thumb into tapered ends of the side shapes to form indents. Using a few dabs of water, attach the three pieces to each other.

B | PREPARE THE CAKES

One 5-inch (13 cm) round tier sliced and filled with butter-cream; one 8-inch (20 cm) square, 2 inches (5 cm) high; three halves of a 6-inch (15 cm) ball cake; and three skewers.

C | STACK THE TIERS

Start with a filled 5-inch (13 cm) round tier and place a prepared 5-inch (13 cm) cake board on top. Add a trimmed 6-inch (15 cm) half ball flat-side down, then another trimmed 6-inch (15 cm) half ball flat-side up through three skewer center supports.

D | FINISH THE BODY

Place the last half ball flat-side down to finish the head. Attach ears with toothpicks and arms with skewers cut to size. (Legs are shown in front of the body where they will be attached after the rest of the cake is iced.)

117

CHAPTER

7

Gallery

SCULPTED FIGURE CAKES

Our Power Puff girl is a sculpted marzipan treat. It balances with the help of a hidden toothpick, just like the elephant on the Ella Fant Dance cake (page 41).

Curious George and some ducky friends are brought to life in marzipan. This cake is similar to the Nutty Squirrel cake (page 44), with the addition of a very simple shell border forming the waves of water.

118

The quilted fondant covering for Little Kitty is exactly the same as the one used on the Blue Birds cake (page 48), and Kitty is made using the same techniques as the birds and the bees from that cake.

It looks like our elephant from the Ella Fant Dance cake (page 41) needed a little break, so here she sits with some friends to say, "goodnight, gorilla."

Here are some examples of cake variations to show how the techniques used for making and decorating specific cakes in this book can be adapted to make your own custom-tailored designs.

PORTRAIT CAKES (AND COOKIES)

Here, the same royal icing portrait technique shown in the Viva Elvis cake (page 60) is used to make Martha's portrait. The bellflowers are from the Monsoon Wedding cake. "It's a good thing."

. . .

This homage to a Paul Klee portrait is hand painted with a technique similar to the Baby Face Cake (page 64), except that the powdered food color (mixed with lemon extract) is painted directly onto the fondant.

Each of these faces was made using the same techniques as the Elvis portrait cake (page 60), except for the piped beads of royal icing used to fill in his face. Here, the outlines were flooded with thinned royal icing to create a smooth finish (Above and below).

119

KATE'S CAKE DECORATING

This little cake shows another way you can mix it up and make up fun cake toppers with unexpected figures and toys, as was done with the model train plastic figures used to top the Jackpot cake (page 80).

Frieda's cake features a gumpaste flower topper inspired by artist Frieda Kahlo, a royal icing interpretation of a traditional Mexican decorative paper banner, and carved vignettes with marzipan good luck symbols in the center tier.

120

Daisy and Mike's cake combines tier shapes from the Monsoon Wedding (page 94), Casablanca (page 102), and the Sammy and Lulu (page 76) cakes, and flowers from the Dogwoods and Butterflies cake (page 85).

This crisp white cake, with just a few flower accents and a vintage bride and groom, mirrors the simplicity of the White Christmas cake (page 73). The groom has been custom-fitted with a marzipan accordion.

The three-dimensional feel of a cake doesn't have to come from the shapes of its tiers. Here the tiers are round, but the small tier is propped on "legs" to form a table with a draped fondant tablecloth. Three-dimensional chairs are made from gingerbread and a carpet of flowers is piped from royal icing (Above and below).

Proving that a three-dimensional cake can be as one-step as a sheet cake, this horseshoe was baked in a horseshoe-shaped pan, that eliminates the carving-the-cake step.

* * *

The Dog Box cake combines the use of a molded character with the cube structure of a three-dimensional cake.

A Few Good Recipes

After years of cake making, these

are the recipes that I've come to treasure. What they all have in
common is that they're versatile enough to be used in project
after project. They provide structure for even the most complicated cakes. Best of all, they're delicious!

ONE DELICIOUS CHOCOLATE CAKE

For years, I never thought I'd find the perfect chocolate cake or the perfect man. Turns out, I found both at about the same time—and I'm sticking with them both! This great recipe has a full-bodied, not-too-sweet chocolaty flavor, and the buttermilk adds a note of complexity.

Makes two 9-inch (23 cm) cakes

2 ⅓ cups (290 gm) all-purpose flour, plus more for pans
1 ½ cups (150 gm) unsweetened cocoa powder
1 ¼ teaspoons salt
1 tablespoon baking soda
1 tablespoon baking powder
3 cups (675 gm) granulated sugar
5 large eggs, room temperature
1 tablespoon pure vanilla extract
1 ½ cups buttermilk, room temperature
1 ½ sticks (170 gm) unsalted butter, melted
1 ½ cups strong coffee

1. Position rack in lower third of oven and preheat to 350°F (180°C). Grease the sides and bottoms of the cake pans with butter or shortening and dust with flour, tapping out any excess. Set pans aside.

2. In the large bowl of mixer, sift together the dry ingredients: flour, cocoa, salt, baking soda, and baking powder.

3. Stir in the sugar.

4. In a small bowl, combine the eggs and vanilla extract. Mix into the dry ingredients.

5. Stir in the buttermilk, melted butter, and coffee.

6. Divide the batter between the prepared pans. Bake until set around the edges and a toothpick inserted in the center comes out clean, about 50 minutes.

7. Transfer pans to a wire cooling rack. Let the cakes cool completely in their pans before removing. Loosen sides of cakes by running the flat side of a knife blade around the sides of each pan. Invert onto wire rack top-side down and remove the pan. Reverse the layers by turning them top-side up again for cooling, to prevent layers from splitting.

Cover in plastic wrap and refrigerate for up to a week. Or, add a layer of foil over the plastic wrap and freeze for up to two weeks.

TIP

◆ For preparing baking pans, I find vegetable shortening and flour best. Many people line the pans with parchment paper, but I prefer not to take the time. There are also nonstick aerosol sprays with flour that can be magically effective.

ONE-TWO-THREE-FOUR BUTTERCAKE

Best known as the 1-2-3-4 Cake for its basic composition: 1 cup butter, 2 cups sugar, 3 cups flour, and 4 eggs. Perhaps also for the fact that it's a snap to make and disappears just about as fast as it's dished out.

Makes two 9-inch (23 cm) cakes

3 cups (375 gm) sifted all-purpose flour, plus more for pans
1 tablespoon baking powder
½ teaspoon salt
1 cup (2 sticks; 225 gm) unsalted butter, room temperature
2 cups (450 gm) granulated sugar
4 large eggs, lightly beaten, room temperature
1 cup milk, room temperature
1 teaspoon pure vanilla extract

1. Position rack in lower third of oven and preheat to 350°F (180°C). Grease the sides and bottoms of the cake pans with butter or shortening and dust with flour, tapping out any excess. Set pans aside.

2. In a large bowl, sift together the dry ingredients: flour, baking powder, and salt.

3. In the bowl of an electric mixer fitted with the paddle attachment, cream butter thoroughly on medium speed until light in color, about 1 minute. Gradually add granulated sugar in a steady stream, scraping down sides of bowl occasionally. Continue beating until light and fluffy, about 4 to 5 minutes.

4. Add eggs into the butter-sugar mixture, one at a time, beating after each addition until batter is almost white in color, about 5 minutes; stop once or twice to scrape down sides. (If mixture looks curdled, stop adding eggs and beat on high speed until it's smooth. Resume adding eggs on medium speed.)

5. On low speed, slowly alternate adding flour mixture and milk, a little of each at a time, to the butter mixture, mixing well after each addition. Beat in vanilla.

6. Spread the batter evenly in the prepared pans. Bake about 25 minutes, until the centers spring back when touched lightly or a toothpick inserted in the center comes out clean.

7. Transfer pans to wire racks to cool for 15 minutes. Loosen sides of cakes by running the flat side of a knife blade around the sides of each pan. Invert onto wire rack top-side down and remove the pan. Reverse the layers by turning them top-side up again, to prevent layers from splitting.

Cover in plastic wrap and refrigerate for up to a week. Or, add a layer of foil over the plastic wrap and freeze for up to two weeks.

HUMMINGBIRD CAKE

When people ask me for carrot cake, I like instead to turn them on to this Southern classic. They're always satisfied. This cake may be fast and easy to make, but the results are truly delicious. Since it's mixed by hand, the texture never gets tough—a dense cake that's surprisingly delicate to the tongue.

Makes two 9-inch (23 cm) cakes

3 cups (375 gm) all-purpose flour, plus more for pans

2 cups (450 gm) granulated sugar

1 teaspoon baking soda

1 teaspoon ground cinnamon

1 teaspoon salt

3 large eggs, room temperature

1 cup vegetable oil

2 teaspoons pure vanilla extract

2 cups chopped ripe banana (about 3 large)

one 8-ounce (230 gm) can crushed pineapple with juice

1 cup (125 gm) chopped walnuts or pecans

1. Position rack in lower third of oven and preheat to 350°F (180°C). Grease the sides and bottoms of the cake pans with butter or shortening and dust with flour, tapping out any excess. Set pans aside.

2. Combine dry ingredients in a large bowl: flour, sugar, baking soda, cinnamon, and salt.

3. Add the eggs and oil and stir, do not beat, until the dry ingredients are moistened.

4. Stir in vanilla, banana, pineapple with juice, and nuts.

5. Divide batter between prepared pans, spreading tops even. Bake until golden brown and a toothpick inserted in the center comes out clean, 35 to 40 minutes, rotating pans halfway through baking.

6. Transfer pans to a wire cooling rack. Let cool in pans for 15 minutes before removing cakes. Loosen sides of cakes by running the flat side of a knife blade around the sides of each pan. Invert onto wire rack top-side down and remove the pan. Reverse the layers by turning them top-side up again, to prevent layers from splitting.

Cover in plastic wrap and refrigerate for up to a week. Or, add a layer of foil over the plastic wrap and freeze for up to two weeks.

Cream cheese frosting (page 126) makes a good filling for this cake.

NUMBER OF SERVINGS PER CAKE SIZE

CAKE SIZE	ROUND OR OCTAGON	SQUARE	HEART	HEXAGON	PETAL
6-INCH (15 CM) CAKE	10	15	10	12	8
8-INCH (20 CM) CAKE	20	30	–	–	–
9-INCH (23 CM) CAKE	–	–	20	22	20
10-INCH (25 CM) CAKE	35	50	–	–	–
12-INCH (30 CM) CAKE	50	70	45	50	40
14-INCH (35 CM) CAKE	70	100	–	–	–
15-INCH (23 CM) CAKE	–	–	70	72	62
16-INCH (40 CM) CAKE	100	125	–	–	–
18-INCH (45 CM) CAKE	125	–	–	–	–

For best results, each pan should be half to three-quarters filled with batter. Serving sizes are somewhat subjective depending on how the cake is cut. For a 3- to 4-inch- (8 to 10 cm) high cake, with each slice approximately 1 inch (2.5 cm) wide and 3 inches (8 cm) deep, this table should serve you well.

TWO BUTTERCREAM ICINGS

Meringue Buttercream

Fluffy, silky-smooth meringue buttercream icing provides both a substantial cake filling and a just-right, creamy consistency for decorating.

Makes 4 cups

2 cups (4 sticks; 450 gm) unsalted butter, room temperature

1 tablespoon pure vanilla extract

5 large egg whites

$1\frac{1}{4}$ cups (275 gm) granulated sugar

1. In a mixing bowl, cream the butter. Blend in the vanilla. Set aside.

2. In the bowl of an electric mixer, combine the egg whites and sugar. Set the bowl over a pan of simmering water and whisk continuously until the sugar has dissolved, 3 to 5 minutes.

3. Mix on high speed using the whisk attachment, until firm, glossy peaks form, about 4 minutes.

4. Reduce the speed to low, and add the creamed butter, about $\frac{1}{4}$ cup at a time, to the meringue. Beat until smooth.

Don't worry if the buttercream seems to break down and curdle when the butter is added to the eggs. Just continue to beat it until it smoothes back out to a soft, creamy texture.

Use immediately or refrigerate in an airtight container for up to one week. To restore consistency, bring back to room temperature and stir with a stiff rubber spatula or electric mixer.

Variation

For chocolate meringue buttercream, add 1 part ganache (page 127) to 4 parts meringue buttercream recipe.

TIPS

■ ■ ■

◆ It's easier to separate eggs when they're cold, and since the recipe calls for heating the egg whites in step 2, go ahead and start with cold eggs.

■ ■ ■

◆ Always use a nonreactive (glass or stainless steel) mixing bowl.

Simple Buttercream

This is a good shortcut recipe, sweet and simple. The trade off: it's not quite as smooth or subtle as the meringue buttercream, but many people prefer using it for decorations that call for buttercream because it's more stable.

Makeso 5 cups

1 cup (2 sticks; 225 gm) unsalted butter, room temperature

2 pounds (0.9 kg) confectioners' sugar

$\frac{1}{2}$ cup milk

2 teaspoons vanilla extract (or other flavor)

$\frac{1}{8}$ teaspoon salt

1. Combine all ingredients in a large mixing bowl fitted with a paddle attachment. Beat on medium speed until smooth, about 2 to 3 minutes, occasionally scraping down the sides of the bowl.

Use immediately or refrigerate in an airtight container for up to two weeks. To restore consistency, bring back to room temperature and stir with a stiff rubber spatula or electric mixer.

Variation

For chocolate buttercream, add 6 ounces (170 gm) semisweet chocolate (melted and cooled) to simple buttercream recipe.

■ ■ ■

CREAM CHEESE FROSTING FOR HUMMINGBIRD CAKE

Makes 6 cups

1 pound (0.5 kg) cream cheese, room temperature

$\frac{1}{2}$ cup (2 sticks; 450 gm) unsalted butter, softened

2 teaspoons pure vanilla extract

2 pounds (0.9 kg) confectioners' sugar

1. Combine cream cheese and butter in a large mixing bowl fitted with a paddle attachment. Beat until creamy, about 2 minutes. Add in vanilla extract.

2. Gradually add the sugar, beating on low speed until light and fluffy.

Use immediately or cover and refrigerate for up to four days. Return to room temperature before using.

AN EASY, FOOLPROOF GANACHE

Ganache isn't just a chocolate lover's dream, even though it's a giant chocolate truffle of a filling—it's a cake maker's delight. It makes a wonderful sturdy base coat for a cake that will later be covered in fondant. It's the one thing I can't resist sampling while making a cake. Adding Cointreau gives it a nice orangey flavor and warmth.

Makes 3 cups

18 ounces (510 gm) semisweet chocolate chips (or block semi-sweet chocolate, finely chopped)

$1\frac{1}{2}$ cups heavy cream

1 tablespoon liqueur or flavor (optional)

1. Place the chocolate pieces in a large heatproof bowl.

2. Bring cream just about to a boil over medium-high heat. Pour over chopped chocolate.

3. Cover and let stand 10 minutes.

4. Whisk the chocolate and cream (and add flavor if desired) until well combined; dark, smooth, and glossy.

5. Let sit at room temperature until cooled. To thicken, beat with hand mixer for a few minutes. It also thickens over time as it sits.

Refrigerate in an airtight container for up to a week. To restore to spreading or glazing consistency, heat and stir over double boiler for a few minutes until softened.

PERFECT ROYAL ICING

This smooth, white, hard-drying icing holds its shape when you're piping decorations. It's also used as a glue to connect decorations. It's sensitive to heat and humidity, and also to grease, so keep it cool and make sure your utensils have been cleansed thoroughly of butter and oil.

Makes about $2\frac{1}{2}$ cups

2 large egg whites, room temperature

4 cups (480 gm) confectioners' sugar

Juice of $\frac{1}{2}$ lemon

1. Beat the egg whites on medium speed to loosen, about a minute.

2. Add sugar about a cup at a time, beating continuously until stiff but not dry, about 4 to 5 minutes. Add lemon juice.

Refrigerate in an airtight container for up to a week. To restore to piping consistency, stir with a stiff rubber spatula.

TIPS

■ ■ ■

◆ If icing is too thick, add more egg white; if it is too thin, add more sugar.

■ ■ ■

◆ Don't use raw eggs in icing made for pregnant women, young children, or people with immune deficiencies. Meringue powder, which is available at cake-supply shops, is a safe alternative; the packaging will carry a recipe for royal icing.

■ ■ ■

◆ To make a thinner royal icing for flooding borders, gradually add a little water at a time until the icing has a syrupy consistency.

FONDANT

Fondant is a pliable, doughlike icing that's rolled out with a rolling pin. It's then draped over a cake and coaxed to fit like a glove. Even with fondant-covered cakes prominently featured in wedding magazines over the past several years, the porcelain-smooth finish of rolled fondant still turns a lot of heads in appreciation and wonder. It will keep a cake fresh for several days. Fondant can also be sculpted into decorations like the bow on the 3-D Kitty Cake (page 114).

Makes enough to cover a 9-inch (23 cm) cake, 4 inches (10 cm) high

Recipe 1:

Buy ready-made! It tastes just as good and it's about 10,000 times less work.

Recipe 2:

1 tablespoon unflavored gelatin

$\frac{1}{4}$ cup cold water

$\frac{1}{2}$ cup (150 gm) glucose or white corn syrup

1 tablespoon glycerin

1 teaspoon flavoring (pure vanilla extract will impart a hint of ivory color; clear extracts are best if you want a pure white fondant)

2 pounds (0.9 kg) sifted confectioners' sugar

1. Combine gelatin and cold water in top of double boiler and let stand until softened (about 5 minutes). Heat until dissolved and clear.

2. Remove from heat and add the glucose (or syrup), glycerin, and flavor. Mix well.

3. Place $1\frac{1}{2}$ pounds (0.7 kg) confectioners' sugar in a bowl and make a well. Slowly pour the gelatin mixture into the well and mix until sugar is blended.

4. Use a rubber spatula to scrape down sides of bowl and remove the sticky fondant to a clean work surface. Knead in remaining $\frac{1}{2}$ pound (0.2 kg) of confectioners' sugar, a little at a time until the fondant is smooth, pliable, and doesn't stick to your hands.

5. Roll the fondant into a smooth ball and wrap in plastic. Place in an airtight container in a cool, dry place to set overnight.

If fondant is too soft, add more sugar; if too stiff, add water (a scant drop at a time).

Fondant can be kept for several months sealed tightly in a plastic bag inside an airtight container. Do not refrigerate or freeze. When ready to use, knead again until soft.

POUNDS OF FONDANT PER TIER SIZE

TIER SIZE (3 $\frac{1}{2}$ INCHES [9 CM] HIGH)	POUNDS (KG) OF FONDANT ROUND, OCTAGONAL, PETAL, OR HEXAGONAL TIERS	POUNDS (KG) OF FONDANT SQUARE TIERS
6-INCH (15 CM) CAKE	$1\frac{1}{2}$ (0.7 KG)	2 (0.9 KG)
8-INCH (20 CM) CAKE	2 (0.9 KG)	$2\frac{1}{2}$ (1 KG)
10-INCH (25 CM) CAKE	$2\frac{1}{2}$ (1 KG)	3 (1.3 KG)
12-INCH (30 CM) CAKE	3 (1.3 KG)	4 (1.8 KG)
14-INCH (35 CM) CAKE	4 (1.8 KG)	5 (2.2 KG)
16-INCH (40 CM) CAKE	5 (2.2 KG)	$6\frac{1}{2}$ (3 KG)
18-INCH (45 CM) CAKE	$6\frac{1}{2}$ (3 KG)	—

This table allows for extra fondant to be trimmed from each tier: it's always best to have too much rather than too little. The excess can be wrapped tightly and reused.

GUM PASTE

Gum paste is a pliable, doughlike mixture that can be rolled very thin to make lifelike flowers or bows and can be shaped into berries or banners and all sorts of things. Technically it's edible, but don't expect much: it's bland and cardboardlike. The consistency should be pliable but not sticky; it should snap when pulled apart. It works best when it's aged for a few days.

1 cup (125 gm) gum-paste mix
   (available at cake suppliers, see Sources, page 141)
1 tablespoon hot water
Vegetable shortening, for greasing

1. Combine $\frac{1}{2}$ cup of the mix with the water in a small, lightly greased glass or ceramic mixing bowl.

2. When completely blended, gradually work in the balance of the mix by kneading into a ball. Grease the surface of the ball lightly with vegetable shortening and wrap well in plastic.

3. Place in an airtight container in a cool, dry place to set for 12 to 24 hours before using.

If the paste is too sticky, add a little bit of the powdered mix; if too stiff, add a touch of shortening.

Since the ingredients for making gum paste from scratch are specific to specialty cake-supply stores, and there's no taste advantage for homemade over the mix, the gum-paste mix is a very good way to go.

Gum paste can be kept for several months sealed tightly in a plastic bag inside an airtight container.

MARZIPAN

Made from icing sugar, almonds, and eggs, marzipan has been around for centuries, and it's used all over the world. It's like a fragrant sweet clay from which you can fashion all sorts of figures, fruits, and other decorations. I prefer it to other modeling pastes for its taste and appealingly dense texture. And, I have to admit, I always use ready-made marzipan. It works and tastes great, and it can be found in most grocery stores.

Makes 2 pounds (0.9 kg)

1 pound (0.5 kg) almond paste, cut into pieces
1 pound (0.5 kg) confectioners' sugar
$\frac{1}{4}$ cup (75 gm) light corn syrup or glucose
Vegetable shortening, for hands

1. Combine almond paste, the confectioners' sugar, and corn syrup in a large mixing bowl. Knead the mixture with your hands (first rub hands with a light coating of vegetable shortening to prevent sticking).

2. Shape into ball and wrap well in plastic wrap; place in an airtight container until ready for use.

Refrigerate in an airtight container for up to four months.

Templates

Trace the outlines of the template onto tracing or parchment paper. Cut the template to fit the area of the cake it will be used for.

Pin the corners of the template using straight pins to hold it in place. See Basic Instructions for working with templates (page 35).

Photocopy all templates at 100%.

VIVA ELVIS! (PAGE 61)

JACKPOT CAKE (PAGE 80)

JACKPOT

A | LEAF PATTERN:
Left side

B | LEAF PATTERN:
*Repeat this pattern on the
front and back of tier.*

C | LEAF PATTERN:
Right side

BICYCLE BUILT FOR TWO (PAGE 99)

A | EIFFEL TOWERS:
Make 9 towers for cake (and a few backups, just in case).

B | SCALLOP EDGING: *You'll need four of these scalloped strips.*

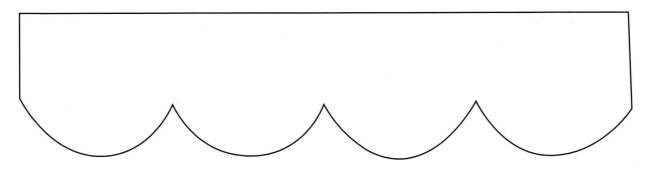

A | PAISLEY PATTERN

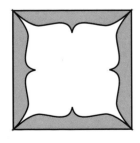

C | LARGE BRACE-BRACKET STENCIL:

Use a tracing wheel to score a checkered guideline pattern of 1 1/4 - inch (3-cm) squares. Copy and use an X-acto knife to cut out the brace-bracket shaped stencils. Line the large outer stencil up within the checkered guides you've scored, trace the stencil with a dark blue fine-line food color marker. Repeat pattern.

D | SMALL BRACE-BRACKET STENCIL:

Center the smaller stencil inside the pattern you've just drawn and trace the stencil with dark blue fine-line food color marker. Repeat pattern.

A | FRONT AND BACK OF CUP: *Repeat this pattern on the front and back of cup.*

WE ARE HAPPY TO SERVE YOU

KATE'S CAKE DECORATING

B | PITCHERS: *Repeat this pattern on the left and right side of cup.*

3-D KITTY CAKE (PAGE 114)

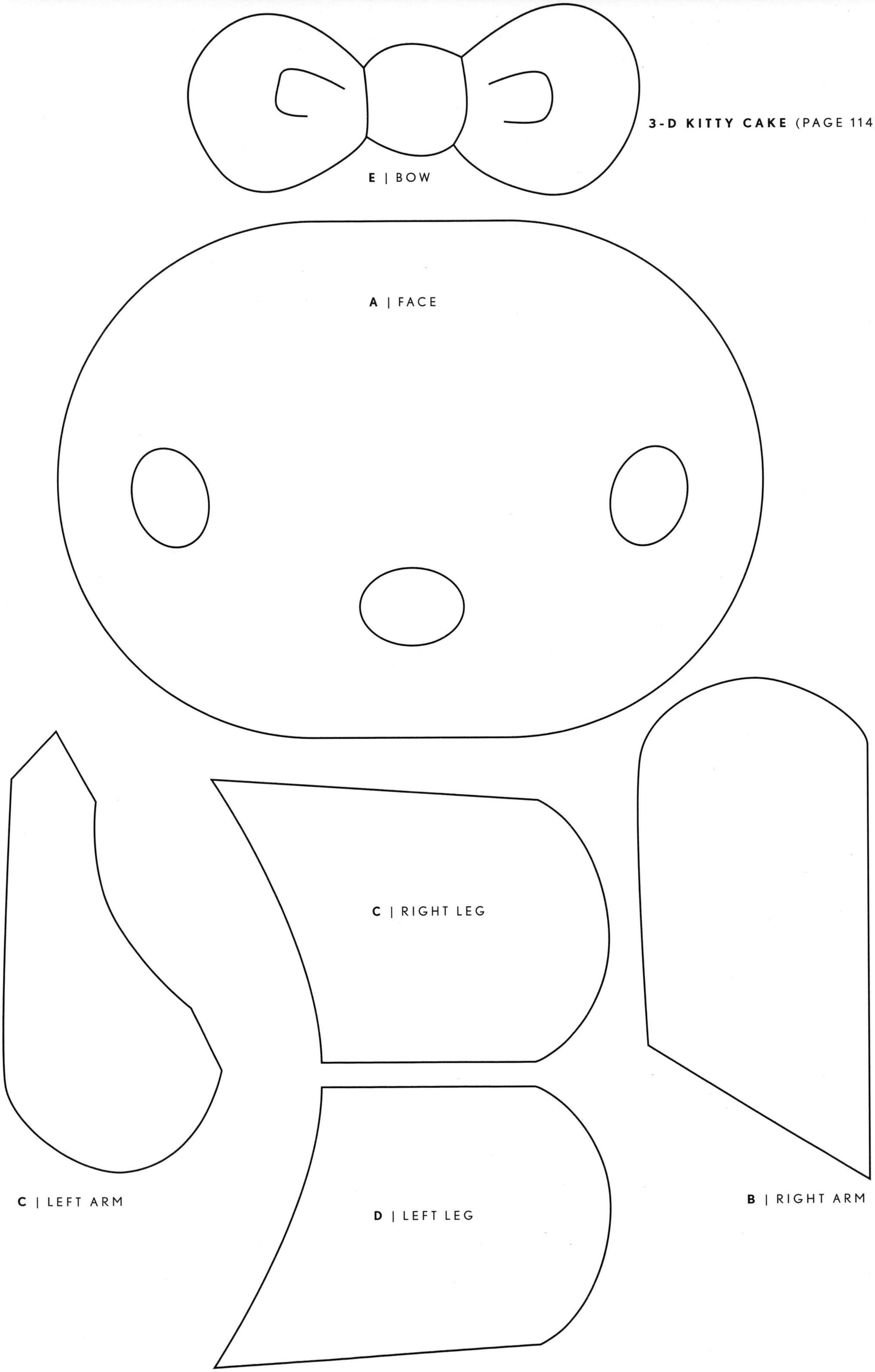
E | BOW
A | FACE
C | RIGHT LEG
C | LEFT ARM
D | LEFT LEG
B | RIGHT ARM

Sources

US SOURCES

BAKING AND CAKE DECORATING SUPPLIES

BERYL'S CAKE DECORATING & PASTRY SUPPLIES
P.O. BOX 1584
NORTH SPRINGFIELD, VA 22151
PHONE: (703) 256-6951/(800) 488-2749
FAX: (703) 750-3779
EMAIL: beryls@beryls.com
www.beryls.com

CREATIVE CUTTERS
561 EDWARDS AVENUE #2
RICHMOND HILL, ONTARIO L4C 9W6
CANADA
PHONE: (905) 883-5638
FAX: (905) 770-3091
U.S. CUSTOMERS: (888) 805-3444
www.creativecutters.com

NEW YORK CAKE AND BAKING DISTRIBUTOR
56 WEST 22ND STREET
NEW YORK, NY 10011
PHONE: (212) 675-CAKE /(800) 94-CAKE-9

PFEIL AND HOLING
58-15 NORTHERN BOULEVARD
WOODSIDE, NY 11377
PHONE: (718) 545-4600 /(800) 247-7955
FAX: (718) 932-7513
EMAIL: info@cakedeco.com
www.cakedeco.com

SWEET CELEBRATIONS
P.O. BOX 39426
EDINA, MN 55436
PHONE: (800) 328-6722
www.sweetc.com

WILTON INDUSTRIES
2240 W. 75TH STREET
WOODRIDGE, IL 60517
PHONE: (630) 963-1818/(800) 794-5866
FAX: (630) 963-7196/(888) 824-9520
EMAIL: info@wilton.com
www.wilton.com

KITCHEN EQUIPMENT

BRIDGE KITCHENWARE CORP.
214 EAST 52ND STREET
NEW YORK, NY 10022
PHONE: (212) 688-4220
FAX: (212) 758-5387
www.bridgekitchenware.com

BROADWAY PANHANDLER
477 BROOME STREET
(BETWEEN GREENE AND WOOSTER, IN SOHO)
NEW YORK, NY 10013
PHONE: (212) 966-3434/(866) COOKWARE
EMAIL: bpisales@broadwaypanhandler.com
www.broadwaypanhandler.com

SUR LA TABLE
1765 SIXTH AVENUE SOUTH
SEATTLE, WA 98134
PHONE: (800) 243-0852
FAX: (206) 682-1026
EMAIL: customerservice@surlatable.com
www.surlatable.com

WILLIAMS-SONOMA
P.O. BOX 7456
SAN FRANCISCO, CA 94120
PHONE: (800) 541-2233
FAX: (702) 363-2514
www.williams-sonoma.com

STYROFOAM CAKE DUMMIES

THE DUMMY PLACE
44 MIDLAND DRIVE
TOLLAND, CT 06084
PHONE: (860) 875-1736

UNUSUAL CAKE TOPPERS

WALTHERS MODEL RAILROAD SUPPLIES
P.O. BOX 3039
MILWAUKEE, WI 53201
PHONE: (414) 527-0770
www.walthers.com
(Jackpot and hat-doffing
cake toppers: G-scale)

PIXI & CIE
www.pixishop.com
Web site is in French, but to get topper
you can email a request in English:
infos@pixishop.com
ALSO AVAILABLE THROUGH:
LES DRAPEAUX DE FRANCE
1-13, GALERIE DE NEMOURS
PLACE COLETTE-75001 PARIS
TEL: 01 40 20 00 11
FAX: (1) 42 97 47 52
(Bicycle and hand-holding cake toppers)

INTERNATIONAL SOURCES

INTERNATIONAL SUPPLIERS

ALMOND ART
UNITS 15/16 FARADAY CLOSE,
GORSE LANE IND. ESTATE
CLACTON ON SEA, ESSEX CO15 4TR, U.K.
PHONE: +44 (0)1255 223322
FAX: +44 (0)1255 223533
Email: sales@almondart.com
www.almondart.com
*Fast mail-order sugarcraft supplies. Over 5,000 sug-
arcraft goodies are available, including consumables,
cutters, boards, equipment, stencils, pillars, ribbons,
et cetera. They also have a wedding favor shop.*

BLUE RIBBONS SUGARCRAFT CENTRE
29 WALTON ROAD, EAST MOLESEY
SURREY KT8 0DH, U.K.
PHONE: +44 (0)20 8941 1591
www.blueribbons.co.uk
*Downloadable catalog. They specialize in sugarcraft
supplies and tools, including cutters, paper products,
edibles, et cetera.*

THE COOKING SHOP
THE OLD ESTATE OFFICES, CHURCH ROAD
SHERBOURNE, WARWICKSHIRE CV35 8AN, U.K.
PHONE: +44 (0)1926 624 444
EMAIL: info@brintonwade.com
www.thecookingshop.com
*Cookware, pots and pans, preparation and baking,
kitchen accessories, et cetera.*

INTERBAKE LTD
UNIT 2, BRIDGE MILLS, ROCHDALE ROAD
BURY, LANCASHIRE B10 ORE, U.K.
PHONE: +44 (0)1706 825 596
FAX: +44 (0)1706 826686
EMAIL: info@interbake.co.uk
www.interbake.co.uk
*Cream machines, metering equipment, ovens, mixers,
pastry handling equipment, refrigeration and dough
conditioning equipment, grills, fryers, stainless steel
fabrications, jelly spraying machinery, et cetera.*

JANE ASHER PARTY CAKES & SUGARCRAFT
22-24 CAKE STREET
LONDON, SW3 3QU, U.K.
PHONE: +44 (0)20 7584 6177
FAX: +44 (0)20 7584 6179
EMAIL: info@jane-asher.co.uk
www.jane-asher.co.uk
*They hold a large and comprehensive stock of every-
thing you need for cake decorating available for world-
wide mail order. They also provide baking equipment,
molds, formers and veiners, packaging dummies, cake
stands, et cetera.*

PIXI & CIE
www.pixishop.com
Web site is in French, but to get topper
you can email a request in English:
infos@pixishop.com
ALSO AVAILABLE THROUGH:
LES DRAPEAUX DE FRANCE
1-13, GALERIE DE NEMOURS
PLACE COLETTE-75001 PARIS
TEL: 01 40 20 00 11
FAX: (1) 42 97 47 52
(Bicycle and hand-holding cake toppers)

SQUIRES ONLINE – SQUIRES SHOP
SQUIRES HOUSE, 3 WAVERLY LANE
FARNHAM, SURREY GU9 8BB, U.K.
PHONE: +44 (0)845 22 55 671
FAX: +44 (0)845 22 55 673
EMAIL: shopinfo@squires-group.co.uk
www.squires-group.co.uk
*They supply over 3,000 cake decorating and sugar-
craft items as well as a range of kitchenware and
appliances online.*

SUGARSHACK
87 BURNTOAK BROADWAY
BURNTOAK, MIDDLESEX HA8 5 EP, U.K.
PHONE: +44 (0)20 8952 4260
FAX: + 44 (0)20 8951 4888
www.sugarshack.co.uk
*Specialist UK-based mail-order company with the
largest online catalog of cake-decorating and sugarcraft tools available.*

SURBITON ART AND SUGARCRAFT
140 HOOK ROAD
SURBITON, SURREY KT6 5BZ, U.K.
PHONE: +44 (0)20 8391 4664
FAX: +44 (0)870 132 1669
EMAIL: sales@surbtionart.co.uk
www.surbitonart.co.uk
*They supply cake-decorating tools, sugarcraft tools,
sugar flowers, ready-to-ice fruit cakes, cake stands,
wedding-cake tops, and bomboniere materials.*

PHOTOGRAPHY CREDITS

ALL PHOTOGRAPHS BY GABRIELLE REVERE
UNLESS OTHERWISE NOTED BELOW:

Holger Thoss, 3; 7 (right); 107
Anna Palma, 9
Don Kinsella, 20; 27 (right)
Darrin Haddad, 2; 118 (top right); 120 (top left)
Jamie Watts, 118 (top & bottom, left)
Anthony Verde, 119 (top & bottom, right)
Jody Dole, 119 (top left)
Andrew French, 120 (bottom left)
Patricia McDonough, 120 (bottom right)
David Levinthal, 122; 129; 140
Kate Sullivan, 119 (bottom left); 121
   (bottom left); 142

Acknowledgments

There are so many people

whose skillful guidance, hard work, and unconditional support made this book possible.

First and foremost, my enormously talented and generous friend Donna Raskin. I would never have done this on my own, but Donna called me one day out of the blue and asked if I'd be interested in doing a cake book. I hardly had time to say yes before she said, "Good, I just pitched the idea to my bosses and they loved it!" Donna's confidence in me has been a constant in my life for the last 17 years, and I can only hope, for the rest of our lives.

I'd like to express my gratitude to my editor Mary Ann Hall for shaping and coordinating all the different facets of this project and guiding me through the creative process. Thank you for your thoughtful and insightful contributions.

The visual presentation is such a huge part of what's great about doing a book like this, and that takes the collaboration of many dedicated, artistic, and organized people. Thank you to my sweet friend, Gabrielle Revere, for taking time away from her busy schedule of shooting supermodels and rock stars and turning her attention to a bevy of baked goods. I count myself lucky to have had such a truly gifted and uncompromising photographer on board (and lucky, too, that she has such a weakness for chocolate!).

Everyone in the Rockport art department has been a complete pleasure to work with. I've long been a fan of the books they've created. I want to thank our very delightful art director, Regina Grenier, and designers at Yee Design, for having such impeccable design sense and for giving the book a clean, sophisticated, yet fun look. Betsy Gammons has been a completely supportive and wonderful photo editor and project manager, always going that extra mile to make sure everything was in place.

A special thanks to the photographers who've shot my cakes for different projects over the years and have openhandedly allowed their photos to be used in this book: Holger Thoss, Anna Palma, Jamie Watts, Andrew French, Darrin Haddad, Patricia McDonough, Jody Dole, Anthony Verde, Don Kinsella and David Levinthal.

Writing is not something that comes naturally to me. Fortunately it's a strong suit for my dear friend, Fred Cohn. He was kind enough to take on the tedious task of reading through the material before it was submitted. Thanks to my wise and encouraging Fred, it seems like I can write real good. Thank you also to Sandra Smith for her special food savvy and expertise in copyediting this book.

To my beautiful mom and family who are endlessly supportive and encouraging in everything I do, I thank you for always believing in me.

And lastly, I am so grateful to my unbelievably lovable, grade-A, #1 husband, David, who, when I said I wanted to quit my day job and become a full-time cake maker, said without hesitation, "That's a great idea, honey!" How do you thank someone who sets up a safety net for you and says, "Go ahead—have your dream"?

Lots of love, and a hundred thousand thank-yous, to all!

Dedicated to the girls: Kelly, Kristin, Kesley, Lauren, and Tara

About the Author

In cake making, Kate Sullivan combines her love of designing and painting with an infatuation for chocolate. Raised in Brooklyn, Queens, and Staten Island, New York, where her personal benchmark for fine cuisine amounted to a Coney Island Nathan's hot dog, she now lives and works in Manhattan (but still gets to Coney Island when she can). For more than 15 years, Kate worked as a director of photography for magazines, hiring photographers as well as casting and styling shoots. She then started LovinSullivanCakes and was dubbed "baker extraordinaire" by *Modern Bride* magazine. Kate learned her baking and decorating skills solely from books just like this one, and has come to believe that, in fact, a really good way to a man's (and woman's) heart is through his (or her) stomach.